Basil's Search for Miracles

—A Novel—

by Heather Zydek

Conciliar Press Ministries, Inc.
Ben Lomond, California

BASIL'S SEARCH FOR MIRACLES
A Novel

Text copyright © 2007 by Heather Zydek
Illustrations copyright © 2007 by Abigail Halpin

Published by   Conciliar Press Ministries, Inc.
                 P.O. Box 76
                 Ben Lomond, California 95005-0076

Printed in the United States of America

ISBN 10: 1-888212-86-1
ISBN 13: 9781-888212-86-0

"Blessed are those who don't see, and yet believe."
—John 20:29.

August

✿ Chapter 1

"I DON'T WANT TO HEAR another word about it, Basil. You *are* going to St. Norbert's Academy, and that's *final!*"

Basil's mother, when provoked, was known to rant and rave; but in this fight between mother and son, the alarming tightness in her tone of voice, her furrowed eyebrows, and the piercing look in her eyes told Basil she was at her angriest. When she reached such a peak of anger, Basil knew it would be unwise to push her any further. In such a state, she might dole out any number of tragic punishments. But with these final, forceful words, he realized the battle was lost. He was, after all, only a twelve-year-old boy. And so it was going to happen: Basil would be attending a new school—St. Norbert's Academy—in only a matter of weeks.

The trigger of this particular feud came in a rather benign-looking envelope. During a rare moment of mother-son bonding, eating cookies and reading books side by side on a rainy Monday afternoon, they heard the familiar clank of their wrought-iron mailbox closing.

"I'll get it!" Basil said, hoping this would be the day the mailman finally delivered something exciting.

Unfortunately, nothing exciting was in the box. What was worse, there was an envelope bearing the logo of St. Norbert's Academy, a school Basil's mom loved and Basil loved to hate.

Basil's mom greedily grabbed the St. Norbert's envelope and tore it open, her eyes fluttering across the words on the single sheet of cream-colored paper it contained.

"You're in, Basil—you got in!" she squealed giddily. Her face was lit up in a way Basil seldom saw—until, that is, she looked up and met the angry flash of resistance in Basil's eyes.

"No. Oh no. I'm not going to *that* school, Mom! You can't make me!" he said, adrenaline rushing through him as if he were charging into battle.

Basil had known this moment was coming, and he had prepared for the fight long before, imagining himself calmly and confidently explaining to his mother with lawyer-like precision why he shouldn't have to attend the stuffy academy against his will. But in the heat of the moment, those well-designed arguments disappeared from his working memory, and instead, an angry sort of babyish blubbering came flowing out of his mouth.

His mom met him with equal resistance.

"Oh, yes, I can make you go to St. Norbert's! I'm your mother, and until you're an adult, I call the shots around here. Besides, I am only doing what I know, as an adult, is best for you."

"Oh, yeah, you really know what's best for me."

"Gah! I'm not going to argue with you about this! I'm three times your age, and I think I know a little more about how to make choices like this than you do."

Basil saw that he wasn't making progress, so he switched from fighting to pleading. "This is so unfair! I don't want to go to a private school! Please don't make me go, Mom!"

"Relax, Basil," his mom said, softening. "Let's talk about this rationally. St. Norbert's Academy is a top-notch school." She sat down on the couch in their living room, massaging her forehead with her hand as if she were getting one of her frequent headaches. "Look, I know you don't want to do this. But your test scores—"

"I know, they're *very* high," said Basil, imitating the exaggerated way his mother said the word "very" while gushing over his scores after they came in the mail.

"Don't mock me, Basil. Principal Wiggins said you weren't being challenged at Mittleton, and with you being as intelligent as you are, you would probably do much better at a school like St. Norbert's. So I don't want to hear you take that tone. Your education is very important to me. It should be to you, too."

"But I like Mittleton, Mom. I don't want to go to a stupid private school, with those dumb uniforms and religious classes and all that."

"Well, I think if you give St. Norbert's a chance, you'll like it. It won't be all bad." She sighed. "Look, Basil, I'm not going to force you to do anything you despise. Give St. Norbert's a chance, and if you can't stand it, maybe we can try something else. But I expect you to at least *try* this school. You got in, which is not an easy thing to do. So I expect you to at least try it for a little while."

Basil still wouldn't have it. "Whatever, Mom. I know you'll make me keep going even if I hate it. You can force me to try, but I'm not going to pretend to like it. Maybe I won't do my homework, or I'll intentionally flunk out. How does that sound?"

And that's when those fateful words came rushing out of his angry mother's mouth. "I don't want to hear another word about it, Basil. You *are* going to St. Norbert's Academy, and that's *final!*"

As usual, his mom had the last word. So he shuffled off miserably to his bedroom—a place he often went to avoid ongoing arguments—and sulked.

BASIL SPENT THE REST OF THE SUMMER before starting at St. Norbert's agonizing over what a new year and a new school would bring. He felt helpless wondering which bullies at the school he would have to avoid, which teachers he would learn to hate, and which kids would be the ones to totally ignore him.

He had a lot to worry about. Basil was not particularly athletic, or outgoing, or even funny. At his old school, he just fit in—he was never the most popular boy in class, or even sort of popular. This was okay—he didn't mind being "average"—but he knew that with a transfer to a new school, he might be picked on, hated, or worse.

The only thing Basil did well was write. He wrote all the time, scribbling away every chance he got in his green, leather-bound journal, anything from short adventure stories to humorous poems about the nastiest kids at his school. But apart from this talent he was mostly a forgetful, disorganized boy, which was a cause of many fights between him and his perfectionist mother.

Basil lived with his mother in a small house in the forested hills just outside a medium-sized city called Mittleton. His mother was an accountant for a small chain of bakeries, balancing books, paying employees, and occasionally even overseeing the production of donuts, bear claws, and focaccia bread if she needed extra cash. She'd never remarried after Basil's father left many years before; in fact, she worked so much she didn't even have time for friends, let alone boyfriends. All she had time to do was work, nag Basil about his grades, his clothes, or his messy room, and then collapse in front of the TV at night before falling asleep. Most workdays were like this, and it put a strain on their relationship, making her angrier than she might have been at Basil's mistakes.

But there were good days—especially on her days off. On those days, she would clean the house, and although this type of thing wouldn't make most people happy, Basil's mom would go about humming like a happy little bee as she got their small house in order. She might even have time to bake some peanut butter chocolate chip cookies for her and Basil to eat after dinner, reading books, crunching cookies, and occasionally sweeping the crumbs off their laps as they read side by side on the couch. Although Basil and his mom didn't agree on much, they both loved books *and* they both loved peanut butter chocolate chip cookies.

Basil's life, for the most part, was fairly normal; and yet he was always slightly unhappy. Something was missing—his father wasn't a part of his life, but it was something more than that, an emptiness. Maybe he was bored, or just lonely. Maybe his mother's nagging over every miniscule mistake he made now that he "wasn't a little kid anymore" and "needed to be responsible" was wearing him down. At this age, he had started wondering why his childhood seemed so far away, so *over*.

All he knew was that he was itching for something new and

exciting to happen in his life. Of course, attending St. Norbert's was not exactly the kind of "new and exciting" he had in mind.

⋅๋๐๋⋅

BUT THEN IT HAPPENED. Two weeks before school, Basil and his mother received St. Norbert's monthly bulletin. His mother, having left for work before he woke, left a note for him on the kitchen counter. "Saw this in the mail yesterday and thought you would be interested. See page 3. Love, Mom."

He noticed the bulletin sitting beside the note and opened to page three. His mother had made a large circle with a pink highlighter around a short article: "*St. Norbert News* awarded Peacock Award for Journalistic Excellence." Just underneath the brief article about the newspaper's award, Basil noticed the bold type: "Award-winning newspaper in need of features editor." The article reported that if any parents had children interested in journalism, they should have them contact Mr. Dixon, the journalism and English teacher, on the first day of school.

Basil's eyes widened. The pressing choice between shredded wheat squares and crispy corn hexagons for breakfast faded from his mind. He could think of nothing but how to get onto that newspaper staff.

To Basil, this seemingly bland news blurb suddenly made St. Norbert's Academy seem like the best thing that ever happened to him. Ever since he was ten years old, when a short story he wrote won first place in the school-wide juvenile authors' competition, he'd dreamed of becoming a writer. While some kids' heroes were firefighters or celebrities or sports stars, Basil had always looked up to popular writers and reporters, and he hoped one day to be like the great journalists he admired.

From that moment forward, he counted the days until school began.

September

⚘ Chapter 2

BASIL'S STOMACH CHURNED as he rode his bike for the first time down the long winding road that led to St. Norbert's Academy. The ride from home to school was a long one, and in the late summer heat, by the time he got to the school his uniform was soaked with sweat.

The private elementary and middle school was a monstrous four-story brick building with three wings, built a century before. It had been renovated ten years back, so the interior was very clean and new, with fancy teaching equipment in each classroom.

The newspaper, *St. Norbert News*, was run by students in seventh and eighth grades. Mr. Dixon, one of St. Norbert's English teachers, was the *News* faculty advisor, and in order to apply for a job with the *News*, Basil had to talk to Mr. Dixon. So a week before school began, Basil had started putting in an envelope the best things he had ever written and typing up a letter stating why he wanted to join the *St. Norbert News* staff. After locking up his bike, he went into the school and straight to the office to drop off his submission before school began.

"May I help you?" said a woman sitting behind a large front desk in the school office.

"Yes, um," Basil said nervously, handing her his envelope, "can you give this to Mr. Dixon?"

"Of course! You must be interested in the newspaper job. We've had lots of submissions!" she said, smiling. "Good luck!"

Basil's heart sank. "Yeah, thanks," he said, his hopes of joining the newspaper staff vanishing as he watched the secretary cram his envelope into Mr. Dixon's stuffed mailbox. Then the bell rang; Basil rushed off to find his first class.

BASIL HAD MR. DIXON AS HIS ENGLISH TEACHER, which was a good thing, because maybe it would help him get an edge over the other students who wanted to be on the staff as well. On the second day of class, Mr. Dixon read the roll call and stopped when he read Basil's name. He looked up.

"Basil Gold?" he said.

"Yes?"

"I'd like to talk to you after class."

"Sure," Basil said, trying to stay calm. Usually talking to a teacher after class was *not* a good thing, but in this case, Basil hoped beyond all hopes that Mr. Dixon was going to tell him he had gotten the newspaper job.

Basil watched every move the second hand made on the clock, anticipating the moment the bell would ring. Finally it did, and the students scurried off, jabbering away. Basil slowly gathered his things, trying to look busy. Mr. Dixon walked up to him.

"So you're Basil?"

"Yeah."

"Nice to meet you. I read your writings that you submitted, and I'd like you to come to our newspaper staff meeting this Thursday after school. I haven't made a formal announcement yet, but when I read your submissions I knew you were the one we needed for our staff. We meet in this room, immediately after the last bell rings. Can you make it?"

"Yeah! That sounds great, Mr. Dixon."

"Good! I'm looking forward to it. Make sure you bring a notebook that you don't use for class. It will come in handy."

For the rest of the day Basil daydreamed through his classes, scribbling notes and ideas into his journal, hoping he could live up to Mr. Dixon's expectations.

Chapter 3

"ORDER, ORDER EVERYONE," Mr. Dixon said, pretending to be a court judge as he banged his fist on his desk. "Let's get this meeting started."

"Aw, do we have to?" said one of the staffers, an eighth-grader named Scott.

"Yes, Scott, we have to," Mr. Dixon said. "Now, first things first. As you all know, we lost Nate last year when he graduated, so we had a big hole in our staff to fill. I had the school make an announcement in the newsletter that goes out to parents saying we were looking for a new staff member. I'm telling you, a bunch of kids wanted this position, more than we've ever had before— you should be proud of our reputation. But anyway, I read all the submissions and this kid here," he said, walking over to Basil and putting his hand on his shoulder, "is our newest staffer. Say hello to Basil."

"Hello, Basil," they said in a sing-songy way.

"Hey," he said shyly.

"Basil here is not only new to our staff—he's new to St. Norbert's. Where did you used to go to school, Basil?"

"Mittleton South," he said.

"Oh wow! That's where I went for my first year of middle school," said Graciela, another eighth-grader and the paper's chief copyeditor.

"Really?" said Basil.

"Well, I think you're going to love St. Norbert's," said Mr. Dixon.

"Yeah, right," said a seventh-grade staffer named Christian with more than a hint of sarcasm in her voice.

"Christian," Mr. Dixon said, "let's turn the attitude down a notch, OK?" Christian always had some kind of infuriating opinion about everything, which made her, everyone had to admit, an ideal opinions editor for the paper.

"Now let's get down to business," Mr. Dixon said. "Let's hear some story ideas. Everyone, take out your notebooks."

Story ideas? Basil had no concept of how to come up with story ideas for a newspaper. He figured he would look busy writing notes and hope an idea would strike him.

"I'm working on a roundup of all the summer movies," said Agnes, the third eighth-grade *News* staffer. "I told the people at Mittleton Cinema that I was going to write about summer movies in the paper and they let me in for free to any movie I wanted."

"No way!" said Scott, practically foaming at the mouth.

"Yeah, I think I saw just about everything my mom would let me see. It was great."

"Good, good," said Mr. Dixon. "What about you, Sarah? Had any good news ideas yet?"

"Well, I was thinking of doing a story about the new addition they put on the school over the summer—the new auditorium and all that," said Sarah, the news editor for the paper. "Is that okay with you? I mean, I don't want to cover it if someone else wanted to. Was anyone else interested in doing that? I really don't want to take someone else's story. I mean, I've actually already spoken with Principal Fishburn about it, but—"

"Sarah, I think it sounds great. The story's all yours," Mr. Dixon said. "See if you can talk to some of the students about what they think of the new addition."

"Oh, oh, Mr. Dixon," interrupted Shamus, the sports writer, "I just wanted to tell you before I forget, we won the first baseball game of the season, and I was going to write about that, since I was at the game on Tuesday."

"Good news, Shamus! That sounds great. What about you, Christian?" Mr. Dixon asked.

"I'm going to do an opinion piece on the controversy over our uniforms," said Christian. Some of the kids were starting to rebel against wearing uniforms, and Christian loved a good controversy.

"Hmm . . . the continuing uniform saga," said Mr. Dixon. "Just be careful with that one, Christian. You know how strong people's opinions are on that subject. Make sure you try to show all the different perspectives before you say what you think personally."

"Okay," she said.

"And Abbie, what are you working on?" Abbie was in charge of finding local businesses to advertise in the paper—this gave *St. Norbert News* a large part of the money it needed to keep printing new issues.

"I went around over the summer and talked to a lot of different stores in town about doing ads with us," she said. "I got about ten new stores who want to place ads!"

"Fantastic!" said Mr. Dixon. "That will really help our budget."

"Oh, Mr. Dixon," said Sarah, "I'm also working on a profile of Mr. Schultz, the math teacher. Is that okay?"

"Sure, Sarah. We can certainly use that, too."

"Basil, do you have any ideas?" Mr. Dixon asked. All eyes were on Basil.

"Uh, I'm kinda thinking about it," he said.

"I'll think, too. We'll all try to think of an assignment for you to get your feet wet, okay?"

"Yeah," said Basil.

Basil was excited to work with Mr. Dixon and the *News* staffers. That is, almost all of them. Anthony—an utterly forgettable character—provided the *News* with dozens of drawings and graphics. Anthony was as much a flimsy wreck as the pink, rust-encrusted girl's bike he rode to school. He was a pale, skinny boy with a mop of straw-colored, unbrushed hair. No one spoke to him, so no one really knew how he was able to go to St. Norbert's in the first place. Some of the snootier students whispered that he was let in as an act of charity.

But because the *News* kids didn't want to be associated with him, they ignored poor Anthony completely, always keeping their distance—with the exception of Sarah, who often felt sorry for him. Of course, it wasn't hard for Anthony's peers to avoid him— he rarely said a word to anyone, anyway.

Despite Anthony, Basil was very happy to meet his fellow staffers. Things were looking up; the *News* staffers liked him. This was a very good thing, in Basil's mind—it meant he had instant friends at his new school.

⁛

MR. DIXON TOOK BASIL UNDER HIS WING RIGHT AWAY. Dixon was young, with large glasses and thinning brown hair. He had olive skin, a somewhat unkempt beard, dark, soft eyes and a pudgy nose. He had once been an accomplished journalist who burned out on his job and turned to teaching. He loved his students and they loved him. Not only was Mr. Dixon the advisor for the school paper, but he was also everyone's favorite English teacher. Only he could spark discussions in his classes that made everyone talk; only he could encourage people to read books one to two levels beyond the typical reading level for a middle-schooler. His students always got grades a little higher than every other English teacher's students; they worked hard, but they had fun.

After the first newspaper meeting, Basil waited until all the other staffers had cleared out of the classroom where they had their meeting so that he could talk to Mr. Dixon alone.

"Mr. Dixon, thanks for letting me join the staff," he said.

"No problem, Basil. I'm excited about what you're going to bring to our paper."

"Hey, I have a question," Basil said. "I've written short stories before, but I haven't really written for a newspaper. How can I learn more about journalism?"

"Hmm . . . you're very young, Basil," Mr. Dixon said, "but I can tell by your wit that you are ready to be challenged to jump to the next level of writing. You're not going to be the kind of journalist who writes just *anything*. You're going to do something special. I can feel it. So here, take some of these books home with you." He walked over to a large bookshelf beside his desk and pulled off a couple of journalism books, handing them to Basil. "Read through them over the next few weeks. And write as much as you can. Write in a journal about the things you do each day. Write short stories. Write about things you hear about in the world on the evening news. Practice, practice, practice. Okay?"

"Okay, Mr. Dixon," Basil said excitedly.

❁ Chapter 4

THINGS IN BASIL'S EARLY DAYS AT ST. NORBERT'S might have been near perfect if it weren't for the story idea Mr. Dixon conjured up for Basil.

"Basil," Mr. Dixon said near the end of the second meeting, "can I talk to you for a minute?"

"Sure," Basil said, stepping away from a conversation with Shamus and Christian about the uniform controversy.

"I just want to say that I think you're going to do a great job with this paper," Mr. Dixon said.

"Thanks," Basil said, feeling his cheeks turn red.

"So I have a suggestion for our paper, and for you," Mr. Dixon continued. "I was thinking it might be a good idea to try something new this year. This is a quality paper for a quality parochial school. What's the key word there? Parochial. This is a Christian school, and to me that means we have a duty to fulfill our readers' spiritual needs as well as their need for news. I just don't think *St. Norbert News* has really lived up to that part of things in the past."

Everyone at St. Norbert's knew, and had forewarned Basil, that as great as Mr. Dixon was, he had a preachy side. He often used to talk of how he had studied to become a priest at one point before becoming a journalist.

"So anyway," he went on, "I'm proposing that we make a serious effort to include more religion-oriented writings into our paper. I want something that will be inspiring, but original— something that would make St. Norbert proud."

Christian and Shamus stopped their conversation and gave Basil a pitying glance. They knew what was coming—Dixon

19

had given them all the "St. Norbert Speech" dozens of times.

"Do you know much about St. Norbert, Basil?"

Basil shook his head.

"He was a man of the world who enjoyed indulging himself in many ways. He became a priest, although he was still immersed in his worldly, godless activities."

Basil wasn't sure he understood why "worldly" was a bad thing, but he continued to listen in silence, hoping Mr. Dixon's sermon would end soon.

"Well, one day Norbert was riding his horse when a stroke of lightning scared the animal. The horse bucked him and Norbert was thrown into the air, knocked out when he hit the ground. Well, Basil, something mysterious about that experience changed him, because after that he devoted himself to the service of God."

Christian rolled her eyes.

"He spent the rest of his life living in poverty and serving God with great zeal." Mr. Dixon was getting emotional—he even seemed a little choked up. "Ah, to be like the great St. Norbert—I love that man. He is an amazing saint, Basil."

Mr. Dixon cleared his throat. They all sat in silence, awkwardly staring at each other.

"At any rate, I want to offer the St. Norbert's student body some kind of spiritually enlightening reading material in the *St. Norbert News*. It is only right for us to honor our newspaper's namesake, don't you think?"

Basil didn't know what to say. He had no idea of how to approach this new challenge. But before he could say anything, Mr. Dixon continued.

"Basil, I know this may be a new topic for you, but I believe you are smart enough and creative enough to do something really interesting. I want you to think long and hard about this and come up with some ideas for our next meeting."

Basil wondered how he could possibly achieve what Mr. Dixon wanted. Basil knew nothing about religion, but he didn't want to disappoint the teacher who had so highly praised him. So he reluctantly agreed to take on the challenge, even though he was half ready to quit *St. Norbert News* before the first issue.

·ॐ· Chapter 5

ALL THE SEVENTH-GRADE *NEWS* STAFFERS ate lunch together every day, with the exception of creepy Anthony, of course, and Abbie, who ate at her more popular friends' table. It was here, on Friday after the second *News* meeting, that Basil brought up Mr. Dixon's request.

"So, what do you think?" he asked the others, trying to keep his salami sandwich in his mouth as he spoke.

"All I can say is this is pretty stupid," Christian said. "I don't think anyone cares that our paper isn't religious. I know I don't."

"We *are* at a religious school, Christian," Shamus said.

"Well, I really need to figure this out," Basil said. "Mr. Dixon is expecting me to do something."

"Basil, if you want, I'll write something," Sarah said. "I have lots of ideas."

"Like?" said Christian.

"Well, like, I was thinking for the first one I could write an article about how Jesus loves us, and how He died for our sins."

"Oh, please," said Christian, "you are joking, right? If you write that, everyone will think our newspaper is a big joke. I think that's a stupid idea." Christian didn't seem to care that Sarah looked hurt.

"So what do you suggest, Christian?" Shamus asked.

"I don't know. It'll be hard to come up with something good. My dad says religion is silly, and—"

"If religion is silly, then your dad must be pretty stupid to send you to a religious school."

"I go to this school, like lots of kids here who aren't religious, because my parents want me to have a quality education, and St.

Norbert's is one of the best schools in town. So in that case, why do *you* go here, Shamus?" Christian said with a fake-sweet smile.

"Can you just get to the point?" Shamus retorted. "No one cares what you think, Christian."

"Well, if you don't care, then why should I tell you?" she replied.

"Just spit it out, Christian," said Basil, getting annoyed.

"Okay, I was thinking, what does interest me is all the mysterious stuff, like hauntings and cults and other weird, unexplainable phenomena like that."

"And you think Mr. Dixon would let us publish articles on cults and demons for our religion column?" Basil asked.

"Yeah, I'm thinking *no way,*" said Shamus matter-of-factly, glaring at Christian.

"Well, he might not," Basil said, an idea brewing in his head, "but maybe Christian's idea isn't all bad. Maybe she's onto something."

"How so?" Christian asked.

"Well, what if we wrote about strange religious stories that aren't as spooky as all that other stuff?"

"Like what?" asked Sarah.

"Hey, you know what?" Shamus said eagerly. "My mom was telling me about a weeping icon in town, at some church around here."

"What do you mean by 'weeping icon'?" Basil asked.

"Like a religious picture that cries real tears."

"Oh, yeah, I think I've heard of that happening," Basil said. "Do you know what church has it?"

"I think it's that one with the big dome. Holy Something-or-other," Shamus said. "Downtown."

"Is it called Holy Resurrection?" Sarah asked. "I think I know which one you're talking about."

"Actually," Christian butted in, "I think it has potential—the idea, I mean, it might be kind of cool. Now that I think of it, I saw something on TV a while ago about stuff like that. They showed all these different miracles and scientists tested them."

"What happened?" asked Shamus.

"I don't really remember," Christian said. "Well, let me think. I remember they talked about a few ideas and basically didn't come to any real conclusion either way. They 'let the viewers decide.'"

"So what did you decide?" said Basil.

"What do you think?" she said with a smirk.

"Well, anyway," Basil said, "maybe what I can do is find the church and interview someone who witnessed it, and then write about it."

"I like that, actually," said Sarah. "You can write the article as a news story and leave it up to the reader to decide what to think."

"Let's ask Mr. Dixon next Thursday and see what he says," said Basil.

Basil was doubtful about the icon, and scared to death to go to a strange church with a crying picture, whether it was real or not. He secretly hoped Mr. Dixon would give him something easier to write about.

Chapter 6

IT TURNED OUT THAT MR. DIXON loved the idea of a story on a local "miracle." He said Basil might run into some challenges in writing it, since it was a very ambitious project for such a young journalist. But Basil was determined to be a *real* reporter, so as daunting as the task seemed, he immediately set to work. His first task: getting his mom's permission to go to the church and see the icon for himself.

"Hi Mom," Basil said on a sunny September Saturday as his mother was preparing to go to work. She often worked on Saturdays.

"Hi, Basil," she said as she put her shoes on. "Did you remember to clean the kitchen after breakfast? I don't have time to do that right now—I was supposed to be at work five minutes ago."

"Oh, yeah, it's done. I even loaded the dishwasher." It was true—he had cleaned the kitchen until it sparkled, hoping to get his mom in a good mood so she would let him go to the church. "Oh, hey, before you leave, can you drop me off at this church in downtown Mittleton? I'm going to write an article about a weeping icon, and—"

"Are you serious? Basil, you know I don't have time to drive you," she said, looking frantic as she searched for her car keys. "Why didn't you ask me about this a week ago?"

"I wasn't really sure what I was going to write on until yesterday," Basil said, feeling a fight coming on. "Well, if you can't drive me, can I ride my bike there? I promise I'll come straight home after. I'll call you as soon as I get there."

"Are you crazy? There is no way I'm going to let you ride your bike all the way downtown while I'm at work. Can't I just take you next week, when I'm not working?"

"My deadline is next week, Mom. Can I take the bus? That's pretty safe."

"No—the answer is no. Why don't you just call them and ask them to describe the icon. Then next time you have an article, plan ahead and tell me *in advance* when you need help from me." She looked at her watch. "Shoot! I gotta go. Mrs. Covello is going to kill me if I'm more than fifteen minutes late. Just stay in the house today, Basil, and do your homework," she said as she rushed out the door.

"Arrrgh!" Basil growled as the door slammed shut. He stomped over to the phone book and dragged it out, thumbing through until he found the address and phone number for Holy Resurrection Church. He took out a map and looked up the address—it was definitely within biking distance. His mom was going to be working for eight hours—surely she wouldn't notice if he were gone for a few hours. He would just tell her that he'd called the church and they had given him the information over the phone.

Basil looked out the window to see if his mother was gone—and then he ran to the garage, pulled out his bike, and rode in the direction of downtown Mittleton.

The church was hard to miss—it was a tall, narrow old building with three onion-shaped gold domes and a bell tower on top. The sides of the building were covered with ivy. Basil parked and locked his bike, walked up the brick steps to the front door, tugged the heavy door open and stepped inside.

Immediately he was greeted by the intense smell of roses, or at least, that's how he later described it to his friends. The church was dark. When his eyes adjusted to the small amount of light provided by flickering candles, he realized that he was in a very unusual place, unlike any place he had ever seen.

Despite the fact that he was in a church, it didn't look like any of the churches on TV or in movies, or like the generic churches he and his mother went to on Christmas and Easter. There were no pews or pulpit. The only things he saw in the vast open space inside the church were hundreds of eyes staring at him.

Those eyes, he soon realized, were on rows upon rows of paintings going all the way up to the ceiling—a wall of paintings, you might say, with a door in the middle. And even the door had a painting on it. The paintings themselves were strange. They were mostly of people dressed in robes. All the people had big eyes. The people stood alone on mostly plain backgrounds with foreign letters written on them.

It was then that he caught sight of the painting just to the left of the door in the middle, surrounded by dripping beeswax candles and vases of tall white lilies. He looked closer and noticed that the woman in the painting had streams of liquid flowing from her eyes and down her cheeks. The liquid eventually rolled down off the painting and onto the floor, where a cotton cloth was laid to catch it.

It was the weeping icon!

Basil suddenly felt a range of feelings, from excitement to a nauseating, overwhelming fear. The eerie, dark warmth inside the church, the large eyes staring back at him—everything gave him a feeling that made the hairs on his arms prickle. It was fascinating and yet terrifying to think that a piece of painted wood could cry. In general Basil found that the church itself made him very uncomfortable. Still, while he was scared standing in that candlelit church in front of the weeping icon, he felt as excited as anyone about to encounter something very strange and mysterious. He pulled a small camera Mr. Dixon had lent him out of his bag and snapped a shot, hoping that the flash would make up for the darkness in the church.

"Our services are over today until Vespers this evening." An old man's voice crackled behind him just after he snapped the shot. Basil's heart jumped. He turned around quickly to see who had spoken. "That's why it's so dark in here. We end the service by turning out the lights. Why don't I turn on the lights for you, so you can get a better picture?"

"Okay, thanks," said Basil.

The person who spoke was a very old man with tawny-brown

skin, soft, black-brown eyes, a long white beard and white hair. He wore a black robe and a huge golden cross around his neck. And his beard—it was possibly the longest beard Basil had ever seen. The man was also very short—only a few inches taller than Basil.

"Are you a priest?" Basil asked, feeling shy.

"Yes, I'm Father Maximos," said the old man. "What is your name?"

"Oh, uh, my name's Basil," he said.

"Basil! A beautiful name—just like the wonderful Saint Basil the Great—one of the fathers of our church. He was a very important leader in the days when the church was only beginning. So what can I help you with, young Basil?"

"I came here to see the icon," Basil said. "I'm writing a story about it for my school paper."

"Ah . . . a curious young journalist. Once I was like you. Always testing, always searching and researching. Looking for truth. You want to see things for yourself, right?"

Basil couldn't take his eyes off the icon.

"Why don't you go look, up close?"

Basil pulled out his notebook and went over to the icon, scribbling down what it looked like. The woman in the painting was very plain-faced but not ugly. Her hair was covered with a hood and her eyes were huge and almost sad-looking. She held a boy in her arms. The boy was small but he had a strange face, almost like the face of a man. Tears streamed down the faces of both the boy and the woman.

Basil tried to look behind the icon. He peeked through the door in the middle of the wall and saw that the other side of the icon was bare—no tubes or wiring could be seen.

"How do you know it's real?" Basil asked Father Maximos.

"Do you see pipes? Do you see any wires at all? Do you see the ceiling dripping onto the icon? If you'll notice, there is nothing that would tell us that someone had fixed it to cry, or that this happened by accident. Skeptics say that the 'tears' appear from condensation. But the icon doesn't appear to be sweating from humidity—otherwise, the whole thing would be wet, and so would all the other icons. There would be no tears trailing down the faces in this one icon. Also, the tears have a fragrance—condensation on wood typically doesn't smell sweet or flowery like that—it smells like moldy wet wood."

Basil sniffed the air. The scent in the room was undeniable—not overwhelming, but a clean scent, sort of like flower petals in the rain.

"Notice the smell in the air?" said Father Maximos. "It's from the tears. Why don't you come sit down? I will try to answer your questions."

Basil sat on a chair near Father Maximos on one side of the church.

"When did the icon start crying?" Basil asked.

"On Easter Eve, the day before we celebrate the Holy Resurrection of Jesus—that's the name of our church, you know—the janitor was sweeping up in the afternoon, getting ready for the evening service, when he noticed that the icon of Mary, Jesus' mother, was glistening. He looked closer and saw the tears. Immediately he contacted me and Father Herman, the other priest at Holy Resurrection Church, and we came and did an exorcism on the icon."

"An exorcism?" Basil asked, shocked. He thought exorcisms were only for people possessed. "Why?"

"To make sure the icon is not influenced by demons."

Basil swallowed hard when he heard the word "demons."

"If we do the exorcism, and the icon continues weeping afterward, we know it is a sign from God."

"Wow. So, why would a picture cry?" Basil asked.

"It's a mystery. There could be many reasons, but most people believe that when an icon of Mary cries, she is crying for all the evil that is in the world."

"Evil in the world . . . okay," Basil repeated as he took notes.

"Here," said Father Maximos, "let me give you something." He went through the door in the wall that held the icon and returned a moment later with a small glass flask. He handed the flask to Basil. "These are some of her tears, mixed with olive oil. They have been used in the past to anoint the sick, and many people in our area are blessed to have terrible illnesses healed after being anointed with them."

Basil was intrigued by the small glass bottle. He wondered what would happen if he ever tried to use the tears to heal someone. He took the flask, wrapped it in some tissues he had stuffed in his backpack and carefully zipped it into one of the bag's pockets.

"Thanks," Basil said.

"I should get back to work now. I have some phone calls to make and such." Father Maximos chuckled. "But Basil, there is one more thing I wanted to tell you."

"Yes?" Basil said.

"I would love for you to write on this for your school newspaper, but please be careful how you do so. We have tried, rather unsuccessfully, to keep quiet about this miracle, not because we don't want people to know, but because we want to discourage the media from sensationalizing the story. A mystery like this is not really for outsiders, Basil. It is meant to heal us spiritually—not to become a sound bite on the evening news. This whole event has already been enough of a media sensation, and people are missing the point. Our faith is about salvation through Jesus, not about weeping icons and other such miracles."

Basil looked up from his notes for a second and nodded. His hand felt like it was ready to fall off, he was taking notes so fast. When he thought he had written down everything Father Maximos said, he thanked him and made his way toward the door.

"You should hurry. You don't want to make your mother wait for you," Father Maximos said.

Basil looked away from Father Maximos and hastily crammed his notebook into his backpack, hoping to escape before the priest could ask him any questions about his mom or her knowledge of where her son was at that moment. The priest's comment made a paranoid Basil think the old man knew everything.

"Um, yeah, bye," he replied awkwardly, hoping Father Maximos wouldn't say anything more about it. He left quickly, jumped on his bike, and rode home as fast as he could.

❧ Chapter 7

THE NEXT MONDAY AT LUNCH, Basil passed around a copy of the first draft of his first column to his fellow *News* staffers. He'd decided to call the column "Basil's Search for Miracles."

Sarah brought Anthony to sit with them. It was a good thing he was so quiet, because that made it easy to ignore him. And if it weren't for the fact that he reeked of fried onions and cigar smoke, it would have been easy to pretend he wasn't there.

"I'm still not sure what to think," Sarah said after reading through Basil's story. "Don't get me wrong, Basil, your article is really good. But, well, I don't know. If it's really a sign from God, what does it mean?"

"I think it means, like I wrote in the article, that maybe it's a warning to people, you know, to be better to each other," Basil replied.

"Maybe," Sarah said.

"I just think the whole thing is probably superstition," Christian said. She paused for a second, then added, "But it is a little freaky."

"Don't you think it's weird that they can't find anything rigged to make it cry? What do you think makes it cry, if it's just superstition?" Basil asked Christian, getting annoyed with her attitude.

"I don't know. I'm not a scientist. But I'm sure there must be *some* explanation."

"That nobody's ever thought of?" said Shamus as he finished reading Basil's article. "I've heard about weeping icons before, and nobody's ever come up with a good explanation, other than to say it's one of those 'unsolved mysteries.'" He turned to Basil. "Your story is really cool. I like it."

35

"And what's more important, Mr. Dixon will like it," Christian said. "That's all that matters, right?"

"Maybe," Basil said. "I don't know, you guys. I've never seen anything like that before. It was crazy."

Just as he said "crazy," the bell rang. Lunch was over, and everyone threw out their trash and rushed off to class.

THAT NIGHT, BASIL WAS IN A GREAT MOOD. His life, for the moment at least, was complete. Even his mom was in a good mood, and she was making his favorite dinner, beef and bean barbecue bake. He'd turned in the final draft of his article to Mr. Dixon—that meant no more stressful deadlines, at least for the moment. Now all he had to do, aside from a few minor homework assignments, was sit back and wait for the article to get printed. Then the opinions would come back—the best and worst part about having your writing in print. If people liked what they read, they might respond with a friendly letter of encouragement. Of course, if they did not like what they read, the other staffers had warned Basil, they could write some of the meanest letters imaginable.

The September edition of the paper would be released to the student body on the fourth and last Thursday of the month. Basil couldn't wait until the following week's newspaper meeting, when the staff would discuss articles and responses, read letters to the editor as a group, and decide what articles to write for the next edition of the paper.

Basil only hoped the *St. Norbert News* readers wouldn't be too hard on him.

❦ Chapter 8

FINALLY THE LAST THURSDAY OF SEPTEMBER ARRIVED, and the first issue of *St. Norbert News* was released to the students during lunch hour. That meant Basil's first article was in print for the whole school to read. As soon as Basil got to the cafeteria, he passed right by the students lined up to receive dry hamburgers and gloppy cheese fries and made his way to the table where Christian, Abbie, and Sarah were selling copies of the *News*.

"Great article, Basil," Abbie said as she handed him a copy.

"Thanks," he said as he turned through the paper, searching for his name. His column was at the top of page four, nestled between Sarah's profile on Mr. Schultz, the boring head of the math department, and Shamus's report on the first baseball game of the season. Basil started reading.

Basil's Search for Miracles:
The Weeping Icon
of Holy Resurrection Church

By Basil T. Gold

Have you ever seen a *real* miracle?

No, not the kind of miracle where you get an A on a test you were sure you would flunk.

Well, allow me to tell you that there is a real miracle happening right here in our fair city of Mittleton.

But first, let me inform you about why I was searching for miracles. You might think that I am the kind of person who goes out looking for miracles, but this is not so. You see, I'm new to the paper, and our advisor Mr. Dixon asked me to do a column on something religious for the *St. Norbert News*. After speaking with the other writers on our newspaper staff, I decided to do a story about a weeping icon a painting that cries real tears.

I learned that there is a weeping icon in our town, but I didn't know exactly how or where to locate it. So my first job was to find the church where it is. I went to the church, Holy Resurrection in downtown Mittleton, and there, in the dark sanctuary lit only with drippy candles, was the icon.

Just then, the bell rang through St. Norbert's hallways. Basil closed the paper and rushed off to class.

"HE'S HERE!" SARAH SCREAMED as Basil ran into the next newspaper staff meeting and threw his backpack onto the first desk he saw. "Basil, you got *nine* letters to the editor!"

The other staffers were huddled around a desk with Sarah in the middle. All of them, that is, except for Anthony, who sat in the corner drawing. Sarah held up several crinkled sheets of paper and waved them at Basil. Obviously everyone else had already read them—that was evident by all the crinkles, and by the most tattered letter, which was not only crinkled but also torn halfway down the center.

"Let me see!" he said.

Sarah reached over the other staffers and handed him the letters.

"Dear Basil," he read, "I really liked your article on the weeping icon. I'm going to ask my parents to take me to see it. Do you think it will still be weeping next week?" Another was of a similar sort, a student asking if the icon was close enough to visit. The torn letter was from a teacher. Mrs. Santi, one of the religious education teachers, "commended him" on his excellent work as a journalist and his wonderfully inspiring article topic.

The only critical letter was written by a renowned know-it-all eighth-grader named Brandtson; it questioned the icon, suspecting that it was a hoax. He also said that the story wasn't really "news," since the "real" newspaper in town, the *Mittleton Sentinel*, had already written a story on the icon months ago, so it shouldn't have been published in a school newspaper. Basil's shoulders drooped as he read.

"Don't worry, Basil," Sarah said, "Brandtson always criticizes the paper. He doesn't like Mr. Dixon because he once gave him a 'B' on a paper."

"Yeah, you should get used to that," Christian said. "But don't worry. He's just jealous."

"Now, Christian, if you can't say something nice, don't say anything at all," Mr. Dixon said. "Overall, Basil, it looks like your idea was a success. I've already had several comments from other teachers on the quality of this article. You're our new star reporter," he said with a wink.

Basil was a little embarrassed, but very flattered. His cheeks turned red; he hated having attention drawn to him, and didn't know what to say to the others.

"Well, now that this article is out, what should we do for next time? I mean, I'm not sure I'll be able to write something like that again."

"Sure you can!" Mr. Dixon said. "I have faith in you, Basil. Do you have any ideas yet?"

"I'm not sure," Basil said. The truth was that he didn't have a clue—but he fully intended to go back to Holy Resurrection Church and ask the priest for help on the next article. He figured that a church with a weeping icon could lead him to more mysteries and miracles; he just had to ask the priest to point him in the right direction.

"Well, I trust you'll do a fine job. Now kids, we need to work on the other articles for the next issue."

At this point, Basil tuned Mr. Dixon out and starting daydreaming about his future as a successful reporter. After the job he had done on the first article, his dream seemed like a real possibility.

October

∵⊙∴ Chapter 9

THE FOLLOWING SATURDAY, Basil rode his bike back to Holy Resurrection Church, hoping to find Father Maximos and get help with a story idea. He told his mom he was going to ride his bike to Shamus's house. It wasn't totally a lie, he told himself, because he *was* planning to stop by Shamus's after he went to the church. He was sure that if he told his mother the truth, she wouldn't let him go.

Once again, when he arrived at the church, it was unlocked but dark inside, with only a few flickering candles shedding light on the wide-eyed people on the wall of paintings.

"Hello?" he said meekly, hearing his voice echo in the dark, empty church. Silence.

He stood quietly for a moment, gazing again at the weeping icon shedding tears right before him. As his ears adjusted to the silence of the church, he began to hear the slightest whisper. The more he listened, the more he realized he was not alone.

He went up to the door in the center of the wall of paintings and peeked in through a crack. Through it he could barely make out the image of a man dressed in black. Basil looked closer and saw that the man was Father Maximos, and he was praying. The light from a candle in front of him shone on his long snowy beard and wispy white hair. His eyes were closed and his lips were moving fast. He paused for a long time, set the icon down, made the sign of the cross over it, and looked directly at Basil through the crack. He slowly got up and came to the door, emerging in silence.

"I'm so glad you came," Father Maximos said, smiling. He then took Basil's hand and kissed it. "I've been waiting for you to come to me."

Basil didn't know what to say.

"Come, sit," Father Maximos continued. "Let me tell you a story."

Before Basil could say anything, Father Maximos directed him to two chairs on the side of the church, and they sat down. It took Father Maximos a minute to sit down—he was very old, Basil realized—about ninety or a hundred. Then he began telling Basil a story.

"When I was a young man, many, many years ago," Father Maximos began saying, "I was full of doubts about many things. About people, about God . . . it seemed that nothing ever satisfied me. My family was very traditional, and one year they decided to make a pilgrimage to the Holy Land. You see, there was this story of a 'Holy Fire' which lit every year by itself in the ancient tomb of Jesus on Holy Saturday, the day before Easter. It was a miracle, they said. I was doubtful, but curious. I decided to go with them and see for myself if this supposed miracle was real.

"In the Holy Land there are many sacred sites, but none more sacred than the church that sits on the place of the skull—Golgotha. They say it is where Jesus was crucified. It is also the place of His burial tomb and the place where He rose from the dead. And, on top of this, Golgotha is said to be the place where the skull of the first man, Adam, is buried."

"Adam, like, from the Garden of Eden story? That Adam?" Basil asked. He wasn't expecting to hear a story, but he liked listening to Father Maximos talk.

"Yes, this skull, buried at Golgotha, is supposedly the skull of that Adam, some believe. Anyway, it is a holy, holy site.

"So, on the Great and Holy Saturday we went to the church that was later built at this site. We stood with crowds of people squeezed inside the building, waiting, singing hymns, growing more excited by the minute. Then the archbishop, who is most often dressed in beautiful robes and a crown, went to the small chapel within the church dressed only in black, simple robes, holding two unlit candles. Before this, the tomb was searched from top to bottom for things like lighters and matches, anything that might have been used to start a fire. The bishop himself was also searched thoroughly."

Basil sat, listening quietly. Mr. Dixon had told the *News* staff that the best journalists were excellent listeners. He decided, though, to pull out his notebook and take some notes.

"Do you mind if I write this down? This is a really interesting story," Basil said.

"No, not at all. I don't mind at all," Father Maximos said. "Where was I?"

"You were talking about how the bishop was searched," he said.

"Oh, yes. So, when it was time, the bishop entered the dark tomb within the chapel. All was silent. A few moments later, he emerged, each candle lit with a unique, unearthly fire, like none I had ever seen!

"Immediately after he came out of the tomb, there was a roar from the crowd. And then, screams—grown women and men around the church shrieked as their unlit candles lit by themselves with this fire. A woman near me began shaking and screaming after her candle was lit by the fire. Unlit, closed oil lamps around the church also lit spontaneously. I gazed in awe at the lit candles around the room. A few were even putting their faces in the fire. This gentle fire did not burn! It was truly miraculous!"

"Did your candle light with the flame?" Basil asked.

"No, and this was most shocking to me—the fact that my candle, which I had hoped would light with this holy fire, did not light. I think this made more of an impression on me than it would have if it had been lit by the holy fire. Because this told me that something was wrong in my life. It made me realize that I was not immortal, not perfect. And without God, I had no light—I was nothing. My unlit candle before me told me that I needed to stop doubting and start believing."

Basil looked up from his notebook. Father Maximos went on.

"Then the woman next to me, whose candle had lit spontaneously, reached over to me and silently used the flame of her candle to light mine. And as I gazed at the living flame dancing on the candle in my hand, I decided right then and there," he slapped his bony hand onto his leg, "to devote my life to the Source of this Holy Fire—the One True God."

"So what did you do?" Basil asked.

"I began my search for this God by reading and learning everything I could about the Holy Fire. As it turns out, the miracle of the Holy Fire is considered the greatest miracle of the church—aside from the miracle of our salvation through Jesus' resurrection, of course. Written testimonies of the Holy Fire lighting by itself go back to the eighth century, and even earlier. This miracle happens every year at the same time, in the same place! And yet, it is virtually unheard of in this part of the world."

Basil stole a glance at his watch. He really needed to go to Shamus's house, but Father Maximos just kept talking.

"Once, several hundred years ago, some enemies of the believers prevented them from entering the church to receive the Holy Fire. So this Fire of God, so gentle that people bathed their faces in it, cracked through a giant marble pillar of the church. The crack exists to this day. If you are curious, I have a book I could lend you that has a few pictures. Let me go get it." The little old man slowly got up from his chair and walked into another room.

As Basil waited for Father Maximos to return, he caught sight of a large icon of Jesus on the cross. Around him, people were crying. Basil noticed something at the foot of the cross, as if buried under the ground just beneath it.

He looked closer. It was a small skull.

Father Maximos returned and handed Basil the book. He flipped through and saw that there was, as Father had said, a large cracked pillar in the church. He also saw a picture of a man holding his face in the spreading flame of his candle. Another picture was of a misty-looking light in the center of the church, an indefinable blur floating in the air. It was chilling. As he looked at the pictures in the book, he felt a strange swelling feeling inside his chest, like he was about to burst into tears.

Father Maximos sighed. "And so here I am, over seventy years later, serving as a priest at this church, blessed to be in the presence of a weeping icon. To God be the glory. So, what brings you here, my son?"

Basil could hardly even remember why he came, but after a second, he remembered—the second article. "Well, I was looking for another miracle to write on for my school's newspaper."

"Ah yes."

"But I think I have an idea."

"Oh?"

"Do you think it would be okay if I wrote about your Holy Fire story? I think that would be a good topic."

"Of course you may write of it. But I have only one requirement."

"Yeah?"

"I would like you to send me a copy!" he laughed. "And I still want to see a copy of the other story, on our icon."

"No problem, Father Maximos." Basil looked at his watch again and saw that it was really time for him to go. "I need to get going," he said. "Thanks a lot for the story."

"Certainly."

Basil gathered his things and got up to leave.

"Oh, and you know, Basil," he went on, "please feel free to visit tomorrow for our service if you need to do more research for your articles. Come and see."

⁘ **Chapter 10**

"So Mom, I was wondering," Basil said to his mom as they crunched on cereal in silence, she reading the paper as she ate, "I know this is short notice, but I was wondering if you could take me to that church I wanted to see—the one with the weeping icon."

She looked up from the newspaper. "Well, I have to go into the office a little bit today—I guess I can time it so that I can work while you're there. Okay, I'll drive you. Just make sure you wear your nice sweater and pants—I don't want you looking like a slob at church."

"Cool! Thanks, Mom!"

After breakfast, Basil ran to his room to pick out what he thought would be decent church clothes, got dressed, and then his mom drove him to the church. "I'll be back at 11:30," she said. "Meet me out front."

"Okay, bye!" he said as he got out of the car and walked up the church steps. It was 9:30 in the morning—church was just about to begin.

Even though Basil had gone to different churches with his mom on Christmas and Easter, and had to go to short chapel services at St. Norbert's regularly, he never paid much attention to anything during a typical church service, dozing off or looking at his watch every ten seconds. So for him, going to Holy Resurrection that Sunday was sort of like going to church for the first time.

Throughout the service all kinds of different people flowed in, lighting candles at the front after arriving. Basil stood in the back and watched as Father Maximos and what must have been Father Herman—the other priest, who was younger than Father

Maximos—and several boys dressed in white robes with golden crosses stitched on them came in and out of a side door on the icon wall, carrying candles. Basil wondered what it would be like to do what they were doing. He wanted to be able to go with the priest inside that mysterious door.

As Father Herman walked around he carried a small gold bowl with a lid hung on a long chain with bells on it. When he walked he would swing the object in different directions. Each time he swung it, smoke came out of the bowl. The whole place was filled with incense—so much that you could almost see a haze of it in the air. It was thick and warm, and flowery-smelling. The songs everyone sang were strange to Basil. They didn't sound like any music he had ever heard before. These songs were monotonous and deep, and without instruments. The music, which rose and fell in a quietly dramatic way, was haunting.

The service seemed endless. Everyone stood the entire time, and soon Basil noticed his legs growing tired. When his mind started to wander, he stared at the icons all over the place, especially the ones that looked like scenes from Bible stories. At one point, Basil looked up and noticed a huge dome in the center of the building, just above him. On the inside of the dome was a massive painting of Jesus staring back at him; he had his left arm wrapped around a jewel-encrusted, golden book; his right hand was held up with his thumb and his ring finger pressed together in a strange way. Around the base of the dome were smaller paintings of other people.

After saying a few prayers in unison, several of the people went to the front of the church in a line, singing. As they waited in line, each person, even small children, had their arms crossed over their chests, the way a dead body might have its arms crossed in a coffin. When they approached Father Herman, he dipped a long, golden spoon into a large chalice and fed them each something on the spoon. It all seemed very strange to Basil.

At the end of the service, Father Maximos came out and stood behind a podium in front of the icon wall.

"Good morning, brothers and sisters," began the gentle-voiced old man. "Christ is in our midst."

"He is and always shall be," the people around Basil responded in unison.

"This week we celebrate the great Saint Andrew the Holy Fool, and I wanted to tell you a little story about him, for the illumination of our hearts.

"Saint Andrew, a prophet, once had a vision of a very rich man in the city who had died. At his funeral procession through the streets of the city, Saint Andrew saw demonic creatures laughing, barking like dogs, mocking, and pouring some kind of vile, disgusting liquid on the body of the dead man, whom the city loved and admired. Horrified at the sight, Andrew turned and noticed a young man weeping in the corner. He approached the young man and asked him why he was in such a state. The youth said he wept because he was the dead man's guardian angel, and the man he watched over was an unrepentant sinner. Although the people of the city envied the man's wealth and splendor, he was secretly a liar, a murderer, and a miser who cared only for his money and things, and hated people.

"Let Saint Andrew's vision be a lesson and a warning to us— that in order for us to be saved from such a fate as his, we must love, deeply, richly, caring not for the things of this world—money, success, power—but only loving and serving those around us, and our God in heaven."

Basil found Father Maximos to be a very sweet but peculiar old man, full of strange and unusual stories. After Father Maximos gave his short speech, he returned behind the icon wall, by the altar; then Father Herman came out and made some general church announcements.

When Father Herman was done, the people in the church lined up and went to him as he handed each of them a small piece of bread. Basil moved to the back corner and stood behind a pillar, watching everything and everyone and hoping not to be noticed. He really didn't know what to do with himself—he was still thinking over everything he had observed. Being in such a place, it was almost easy to forget about how different the outside world was, with its bustling traffic and busy people running around from one thing to the next. The world inside this church was strange to him. He felt out of place.

After everyone had slowly cleared out, Basil walked toward the front of the church, where he saw Father Maximos speaking with one of the altar boys. Then the priest noticed Basil.

"Hello! I'm so glad you came. Did you get some good information for your article?"

Basil wasn't really doing research for his article—he was there out of curiosity. But they didn't need to know that.

"Yeah. Thanks," he said.

"I'm glad we were able to help."

Basil didn't say anything. He couldn't figure out how to ask the thousand questions running through his brain.

"You look like you have something on your mind," said Father Maximos. "Is there something I can help you with?"

"Well, I had a few questions about that service, I guess."

"Oh, sure. Why don't we sit down?" He led the way to the chairs at the side of the church. "Have you ever been to a church like this before?"

"I don't think so."

"Where is your notebook?" Father Maximos asked.

"Huh?"

"I thought you were going to ask me more questions for your article."

"Oh, no. Actually, I'm just here out of my own curiosity. I'm not working on an article right now," Basil said.

"I see," said Father Maximos. "Well, what can I help you with?"

Basil struggled to find the right thing to say, trying not to sound rude or obnoxious. But he couldn't find the perfect, sugar-coated words, so he just blurted out what was on his mind.

"Why is your church so weird?"

Father Maximos' eyes widened. "Weird?"

Basil laughed nervously. "Well, like, I mean, why is it so different? This church doesn't look like other churches. The music doesn't sound like other music—it doesn't even sound like church music. The air is so smoky. And the icons all over the place, it's not something you see every day. And it was so long—and how come you guys never sit down?"

Father smiled.

"Basil, you have much to learn. Our church looks different because it *is* different. You see, we are not of this world. We choose to belong to God, and so our worship is otherworldly—it is heavenly. It stands outside of time. This is how our church has worshipped God since the earliest days after Jesus died and then rose from the dead. And even for thousands of years before Jesus, believers worshipped in a way similar to this."

"So you think it's heavenly?" Basil said, feeling doubtful.

"Yes, we believe so."

"Oh." Basil had always imagined heaven to have an endless supply of sweets and cheese fries, no bedtime and lots of whizzing around on magical clouds.

"You will understand more as you learn more, and you will learn more as you experience more. You are only beginning the journey toward Truth. And anyway, my explanations would sound more like ramblings, useless and confusing. I'm afraid I would lose your interest quickly," he said. "In time, your questions will find answers."

"That's okay," Basil said, "I think I need to go start watching for my mom now, anyway. She said she'd be here to pick me up at 11:30."

"Sure, I understand. You should get going." Basil got up and made his way toward the exit.

"Oh, one more thing, Basil," Father Maximos said.

"Yeah?"

"If you can come next week, please talk to me after church. I think I may know of another miracle you might want to write about."

✾ Chapter 11

THE FOLLOWING SUNDAY AFTER CHURCH, Basil went to Father Maximos to ask about the miracle he had mentioned.

"Ah, yes," he said. "What I wanted to tell you is that there is a woman in our parish, Fotini, who was dying of cancer and was miraculously healed after being anointed with the tears of our weeping icon. She was not a regular church attendee; but she came to me a while ago and told me of her healing and how it has changed her life. Fotini is here today. Why don't you go wait in our office—I will find her and send her to you."

Basil sat in the office for a few moments, twiddling his thumbs and gazing at the various items all over the room, from ancient icons to books. Finally the door creaked open. Basil looked up and saw an older woman with short, scruffy gray hair. The woman was smiling as she walked in and sat down.

"Well, hi there, buddy!" she said. "So you want to hear my story? What's your name? I'm sorry—Father never tells me these things," she said with a laugh.

"Basil," he said shyly.

"So, Father tells me you want to hear all about my miraculous healing," she went on. "I'll tell you whatever you want to know."

"Thanks," Basil said. "So you were healed by a miracle? What happened?"

"It *was* a miracle." Her smile disappeared. She looked very grave. "I was a very sick lady—I had two, three days at most to live. This was a few months ago. I had been in the hospital for months and became nothing more than a skeleton. I was all skin and bones, no kiddin'. I know that's hard to believe now," she laughed again as she gestured to her own body— "I regained the weight pretty fast, and *then* some. So anyway, back when I was sick, I only had enough energy to open my eyes and say a few words, but that was *it*."

Basil found it hard to imagine this lively person being deathly ill. Fotini continued, "Finally one day, my doctor told me that I had tumors on just about every organ of my body, some the size of grapefruits, and soon I was going to be pushing up daisies, if you know what I mean. And see, I was scared stiff, because if I died, then who would take care of my iguana? She'd been at my sister's while I was in the hospital, and my sister hates lizards." Basil laughed. But then Fotini became serious again.

"In all seriousness, though, it was the most terrible thing to be in that near-death state—just horrific. But Basil, you see, the terror came not so much from my physical state, but from my spiritual state. My soul was dying along with my body. I was a goner."

"What happened?" Basil said.

"Well, my dear friend Father Maximos, even though I didn't really know him at the time, came for a visit. He was told by a friend of a friend of a friend that I was sick. He came to my room early one evening, just before visiting hours ended. I'd been crying all day—imagine, with what little energy I had. And anyway, tough old ladies like me hardly ever cry. But I knew I was going to die, and I was scared stiff. He said very little, but he was so warm and kind and, well, joyful, even to be around someone on her deathbed. I remember he said some prayers in front of me—and believe me, it came as a shock, since before that moment I was very angry with God because of my sickness—and then he took out a small jar and smeared some oil on my forehead and hands and mouth, praying the whole time. Before I could ask him what the heck he was doin', I felt this, well, this amazing *calm* come over me. I felt such a tremendous peace. In fact, after, I fell asleep."

"So then what happened?" Basil asked, taking notes furiously like a good reporter.

"The next morning was just a beautiful day. I remember the spring sunlight coming into my room. I woke very early and saw green leaf buds on the trees just outside my hospital room window. Then I remembered that I was a dying lady. This was my daily ritual. Wake up to the sun and the green outside, remember my own dying body and get angry, or cry. But on this day, I didn't cry. When my thoughts turned from the beauty outside to my own body, something was different. I felt *healed*.

"So you better believe I called my nurse right then and there— I yanked on that little 'call for help' thingy next to my bed, maybe a dozen times. When she came in, she was shocked to find me sitting up in bed, smiling. 'What happened?' she asked me, aghast. 'I don't really know,' I told her, 'but I feel so much better. Did the doctor give me some kind of new drugs last night?' My nurse said she wasn't sure, and she left right away to find him.

"I spent that morning taking a bunch of tests—X rays and that kind of stuff. At the end of the day, my doctor came in with a very odd look on his face. I couldn't tell at that moment if he was happy or sad. Without a word he sat down by my side and took my hand. 'All I want to know,' he said to me, 'is what kind of miracle happened last night to clear your body of everything that was killing it yesterday.'"

Basil's mouth dropped open. "Even the doctor saw it?"

"Yes, even my famous doctor witnessed the miracle. He said that every X ray and test showed that my body, though weak from its fight with the sickness, was tumor-free. Do you know any doctors, Basil?"

Basil thought of Doctor Lasen, the pediatrician at Mittleton Clinic who always managed to have a long, sharp needle ready to stick in Basil's body at every checkup.

"A few," he said.

"Well, I've seen a *lot* of doctors in my lifetime," she said. "But only one doctor cried at the foot of my bed and praised God for a miracle that even the best doctors can't bring about with modern medicine. And when he did that, it all became crystal clear to me—I was healed through that little priest—healed by God. I was able to leave that hospital a week later, and I'll tell you what, Basil.

I went straight to church to thank God for saving my body, and my soul, from death. And when I went to Father Maximos and told him about the miracle, he told me that the oil he'd anointed me with was mingled with the tears of the weeping icon. That's what healed me. I have only Jesus and His mother to thank for that. And then I went and got Sheila, my iguana, and took her back to my place so my sister wouldn't have to suffer through cleaning her cage anymore. Oh, was Sheila happy to see me. Heh!"

"Here," she said, handing Basil a photograph she fished out of her wallet. "That was me while I was sick."

Basil saw a bony woman lying in bed, her eyes barely open, looking ready to die at any moment, with a healthy woman hugging her. "That was me, that dying woman, with my sister. Can you believe it?"

Basil had to admit Fotini's story was amazing. But he was still something of a skeptic, and a tiny bit of doubt fluttered around in his mind. What if she were making it up, or just wanted to believe it was a real miracle? Couldn't it have just been some really good medicine? Before he could ask, she answered his questions in a single sentence.

"Now come on, I want to introduce you to the doc who took care of me while I was dying."

FOTINI LED BASIL TO THE HOLY RESURRECTION BASEMENT, where the after-church coffee hour was in progress. She took him to a table where a man was eating a donut. He looked like an ordinary older man, with darkish skin, shiny black hair, and a trimmed beard. He was very tall, looming over Basil as he stood up and reached down to shake Basil's hand.

"Hi there," the man said to Basil. "I'm Doctor Raphael. Come, have a seat with us. Have a donut."

"Thanks," Basil said, sitting down next to the friendly doctor.

"What brings you to Holy Resurrection? Are you a relative of Fotini's? She hasn't been bugging you with her prison stories again, has she?" Doctor Raphael smiled and gave Fotini a nudge.

"Hey Doc, thanks, but I haven't shared any of those stories yet with this little guy. There's plenty of time for that." She turned to Basil. "Don't worry, now—I wasn't in prison or anything. I was a prison guard for most of my career. I just retired, actually."

"Oh," Basil said, a little disappointed that he wasn't sitting next to an ex-convict—that would have made for an interesting story. ("Ex-con almost dies from cancer, gets healed miraculously," the headline in his mind read.) "Actually," he said, turning to the doctor, "I'm writing about miracles for a religion column I do for my school newspaper, and after hearing about Fotini's miracle, I'm thinking I might actually write about it. She told me I should talk to you."

"Ah, the miracle," said Doctor Raphael. He suddenly looked very serious. "I'm sure she's given you all the details. Listen, let me tell you something. Before I met Fotini, I never went to church. If you asked me whether or not I believed in God, I would say either yes or no, depending on whether it was Christmas, Easter, or some other day, because aside from on the holidays, when I let my sentimental side loose a bit, I was very stoic, very practical—and most of the time, God, to me, was nonsense. We learned in medical school that we doctors have the power to heal bodies through chemicals and surgery. In my mind, God had nothing to do with it—at least, with the exception of those people who got better by thinking positively, whether through prayer or something else. But let me tell you, no amount of positive thinking was going to heal Fotini. She was a lost cause. I've never seen a case like hers recover." He paused, shook his head. "Never."

"But when that little priest with his long robes and even longer beard came quietly into our hospital that night, something stirred in my heart. And the next morning, when the nurse called to me with such urgency in her voice, any other doctor would have thought the woman was dead. But I knew immediately that it was just the opposite. I knew that she had been healed even before I saw her. And sure enough, she had.

"Have no doubts, my boy," Doctor Raphael said, grabbing Basil's shoulder and smiling. "God is very, very real. I'm a living witness to the reality of His healing. And if God can heal Fotini's body, I have faith that He can heal her soul, and mine, and yours."

Basil's pen halted on his notepad when the doctor said, "and yours." The hairs on his arms stood on end.

As Doctor Raphael spoke, Father Maximos wandered over to their table and sat down, listening to the doctor speak. When he finished, Father Maximos smiled, shaking his head slowly in amazement. "Yes," he said in his quiet, peaceful way. "Such a wonder. God is good." He paused for a moment. "But let me emphasize, Basil," he continued, "that miracles such as this should not lead one to believe that if a very sick person is not healed from cancer, he or she did not pray hard enough. Sometimes, such healing is not a part of God's mysterious plan for us while here on this earth."

"Indeed. Yes, indeed," said Doctor Raphael, nodding vigorously. "I myself have witnessed many very holy people pass on to eternity with a prayer for healing on their lips. Before I was a believer, I used to think this was proof that the God they prayed to wasn't real. However, I now know that although they were not healed on this earth, it was their time to go be with God, who has restored them to fullness in heaven."

Fotini leaned in toward Basil. "Listen to what these guys say," she whispered, loud enough for all to hear. "They know what they're talking about. I know I sure don't!"

Basil nodded, still writing on his notepad and chewing on a too-large piece of donut he stuffed into his mouth between sentences scrawled onto the page.

"Fotini!" Father Maximos said, patting her back and smiling. "You are far too humble! Why, your holiness exceeds us all."

"Are you kiddin'? That's not what my sister says. I'm sure she could tell you in all sorts of ways just how unholy I am. But anyway," she said, turning to Basil, "I'm not one for showing off pictures of myself, but if you're interested, I'll let you borrow the picture of me in the hospital. And here," Fotini said, taking another picture out of her wallet, "take this picture, too, from my retirement party, and you can do a sort of before-and-after photo thingy with your article. I'm sure that'll get the kids at your school going."

Basil was thrilled. Surely this would be his best article yet. He couldn't wait to tell the other staffers that not only did he get a great story, but he also had pictures to prove it.

November

❁ Chapter 12

NOVEMBER CAME AND WENT, and the rolling hills of Mittleton already had a dusting of snow on them from an early December snowfall. Christmas break was only a week away, and Basil couldn't wait for the time off from school. His November-December work for the *News* veered away from the miracles theme temporarily; for November's special "Turkey Day" edition of the paper, his job was to interview different teachers about their personal Thanksgiving traditions with their families. For December, another holiday issue, he had to interview students about what they wanted for Christmas in the ever-popular "Christmas List" section. He had fun interviewing the students, and it helped him get to know them a little better.

"So now that you've been at St. Norbert's for a few months," said Christian between bites of a carrot stick at lunch one day, "wouldn't you agree that it's similar in too many ways to a correctional facility, Basil?"

"Come on, Christian," said Shamus. "It's not that bad and you know it. From what I hear, it's a lot better than Mittleton North and Mittleton South. Their sports teams are awful!"

"Like I care about sports! At least at those schools the kids are normal. Unlike you, Shamus."

"As if you know what normal is, Christian."

"The teachers there aren't as invested in the students' educations—that's one thing I've noticed," Basil said, trying not to spray the food in his mouth all over Christian, whom he had taken a particular liking to. "I mean, the teachers at my old school were nice enough, but here they just seem really helpful. I don't know, though. Aside from the uniforms and the religion classes, I'm not sure the schools are all that different."

"Yeah, religion classes. Don't get me started on that. At least it's entertaining, learning about all the saints who got their heads cut off and stuff."

"I love the saint stories," said Sarah. Christian changed the subject.

"Well, I guess if nothing else you have our great newspaper here," Christian said. Her voice was uncharacteristically devoid of sarcasm.

"Yeah, I know. That's probably the thing I love most about St. Norbert's. Mr. Dixon is the best."

"Yeah, he's great," Shamus said.

"What about us?" Christian asked, batting her eyes at Basil.

"I guess you guys are pretty cool, too."

"Well, we *love* you, Basil. You're our star reporter! People just about died when they read your holy fire story. What's next, I wonder?" Christian said. The sarcasm was back.

"Whatever, Christian. I'm not the star reporter. We all do something important for the paper. Anyway, I haven't had much time to think about what I'm going to write on next. I might write about this woman at Holy Resurrection who was miraculously healed from cancer. But I'm practically failing Mr. Schultz's algebra class and my mom's going to kill me if I don't do well, so I can't think about the article until later. My mom's an accountant, so math is her favorite subject. When Mr. Schultz sent her a progress report last week telling her I was getting a D in his class, she flipped. She even said she might make me quit the *News* if I don't bring my grade up."

"That's rough," said Shamus. "I'm not doing so well in Mr. Schultz's class myself."

Sarah looked at her watch. "Is the bell about to ring? Before I forget, I need to give you guys something. I'm having a Christmas party at my house next week." She pulled invitations out of her bag and passed them to Shamus, Christian, and Basil. "I hope you can come!"

December

✿ Chapter 13

BASIL RAN UP TO SARAH'S HOUSE on an icy cold Friday night and rang the doorbell. He considered himself very lucky that the *News* kids had taken him into their crowd right away, and even invited him to a Christmas party.

A clean-cut, dark-haired man wearing wire-rimmed glasses and a red sweater vest answered the door. "Come on in," he said; he was friendly but a little stiff. "And you are . . . ?"

"Basil," he said, taking off his heavy-duty winter coat, hat, and gloves.

"Basil, hmm . . . now that's an interesting name. They're in the basement. First door on the right."

"Thanks," he said.

Basil went down the staircase to the basement. He was the last one to arrive—his mom got off late from work, so he had to wait for her to get home to drive him to the party. Sarah, Shamus, Christian, and Abbie were sitting on couches, drinking punch and eating cookies frosted and covered with white sprinkles. He went to a table covered with treats and grabbed a cookie for himself, and a napkin.

"Hey, Basil! Look everyone, our 'star' reporter is here," Christian said, mocking Basil as only she could.

"Very funny, Christian," Basil said.

"Anyway, Basil," Sarah said, "you got here just in time. We're about to watch a movie."

Basil hoped it was a good one. He'd had a day full of homework catch-up and wanted to relax. He hoped they would maybe watch a Chet Chin martial arts film—almost all the kids at school were crazy about Chet Chin these days.

Just then Sarah's mom and dad came down the stairs. Sarah's mom had the movie in her hand. Her dad spoke.

"Hi, kids, welcome," he said. "This is a Christmas party, and we're here to celebrate the true meaning of Christmas—the birth of Jesus. We got this movie for you to watch about the first Christmas. I think you're going to love it!"

He set up the movie and then he and Sarah's mom went upstairs quietly. Basil reached to turn off the lamp next to him.

"Oh no, please don't turn off the lights," Sarah said.

"Why?" Christian asked.

"My parents don't think boys and girls should sit together in the dark," Sarah said, looking embarrassed.

Christian elbowed Abbie and they started giggling.

Basil felt a little sorry for Sarah. After all, it wasn't her fault that her parents were strange. He knew Christian could be insensitive, but he was learning that she could also be downright mean. He decided that he didn't like Christian as much as he'd thought he did.

"So, uh, Sarah, where is everyone else?" Basil asked. He noticed that only about half of the staff was at the party.

"I don't know," she said, puzzled. "Maybe they didn't want to come because of the cold."

The movie was very old and quiet. It was hard to tell what was going on, but one thing was certain—it was very long, and very boring. At one point, Basil looked over at Shamus and saw his head jerk up after he dozed off for a moment. Abbie and Christian were whispering and giggling as if no one could hear them, and Sarah, who was sitting nearby, tried to ignore them.

Basil kept himself occupied by glancing around the room at Sarah's things. As a journalist, he had gotten used to observing his environment—you can learn a lot about people, he told himself, by the kinds of things they hang on their walls. Sarah's parents mostly had religious scenes and posters with religious poems and slogans on them, like "Clap your hands and praise the Lord," and, "Jesus is LORD." He picked up a book on the end table called

Biblical Adventures and flipped through it, looking at the glossy pictures on every other page of ancient warriors, kings, and prophets. He was so busy looking at the book that he almost didn't notice when the movie ended. Apparently, nobody else seemed to notice either—Shamus was snoring, and Abbie and Christian were still blabbing, occasionally even scribbling down little notes to each other.

"Um, guys?" Sarah said, getting up to turn off the TV. "The movie's over."

"Oh, hey, Sarah, sorry. It was so boring we didn't notice," Christian said.

Abbie elbowed her in the ribs. "Christian! You're so mean!"

"I'm not mean. I'm just brutally honest. Does someone want to wake Shamus up?"

Sarah had tears in her eyes. It was clear from the look on her face that she was about ready to give up on her "party" and send everyone home.

"Be quiet, you guys," Basil said. "Thanks for the movie, Sarah. It was interesting. Uh—can I have some more punch?"

"Sure, Basil," said Sarah, quickly wiping tears out of her eyes.

"I'm sorry, Sarah," said Christian, trying to get serious. "I'm not trying to be mean. It's just that I've never really been to a party like this before. And your family—well, I guess they're just kind of different, that's all."

"What do you mean, different?" Sarah said.

"Well, like, your parents. They're obviously really, really religious. They're even more religious than Mr. Dixon," Christian said, getting up to take another cookie.

"Actually, my parents used to be pretty different," Sarah said. "When they were younger they got into lots of trouble. Even when they met and got married they weren't religious."

"Really? That's kind of interesting," Christian said. Basil was glad to see her making an effort.

"Yeah. Then my dad lost his job when I was a baby, and my parents were really having a hard time with money and stuff. So a friend of my dad's invited him to church. My dad went, and after going for a few months to Bible studies and stuff like that, he got saved. Then my mom started going and she got saved too."

"Got saved?" Christian asked. "Saved from what?"

"Jesus saved them. You know, so they could go to heaven," she said.

There was a long awkward silence.

"Go to heaven?" Shamus said, stretching (he had just woken up from his nap). "Everyone goes to heaven as long as they're good people. I don't understand what difference it makes if a person is 'saved.'"

"Shamus, nobody is really *good*. We're all sinners. That's what the Bible tells us. We can only go to heaven when our sins our forgiven. And our sins are forgiven when we believe that Jesus died for us. And His death saved us."

Everyone stared at her blankly.

"Oh Jeeze," Christian said. "You sound like those preachers on TV, the ones that tell you how to go to heaven and then ask for your money. 'Save me Jee-zus,'" she mocked, waving her hands in the air.

Shamus rolled his eyes.

"Don't forget the resurrection part, Sarah, you know, that Jesus died and then came back to life," Basil said. Everyone turned and looked at him in shock.

"How do you know about that?" Sarah said. "You're not a Christian, are you Basil?"

"Well, I've kind of been going to church," he said.

Christian's mouth dropped open. "You?! Basil, what happened?"

"Well, after I saw the weeping icon, I started talking to a priest at that church, and he invited me to come back, so I did."

"So are you saved, Basil?" Sarah asked again.

"I don't really know if I'd say that," Basil said. Sarah looked disappointed. "At least, I'm not sure. I don't know what I believe."

"So Basil," Christian said, "Is your family religious?"

"No, not really. I mean, my mom and I never used to go to church. My mom still doesn't go to church."

"What about your dad?" Abbie said.

Basil looked down for a moment, trying to figure out what to say. "I don't know my dad," he said. Everyone was quiet.

"But anyway," Basil said, "What about you guys? Are your families religious?"

"Mine is," Shamus said. "My parents make me and my brothers go to mass every Sunday. I hate church. It's so boring. My parents make us get all dressed up, and like, we can't even leave to go to the bathroom during the service. So my brothers and I sometimes sneak in little pieces of paper and those little golf pencils, and then when Dad isn't looking, we write secret notes back and forth. My mom's not there because she sings in the choir."

"I guess if I went to church every Sunday my whole life, I might think it was boring, too," Basil said.

"I'm with you, Shamus," Abbie said. "My dad and step-mom don't go to church every Sunday, but we go enough."

"Well, we don't go to church at all," said Christian. "My parents don't believe in religion. My dad was raised Jewish, and my mom's parents were Chinese Christians. Actually, my grandma used to be a Buddhist, but she was named Christian when she converted, so even though my mom isn't religious, she named me after her mother."

"I wondered why you had that name," said Shamus.

"Yeah. My dad is really against religion, but my mom is kind of okay with it, because my step-dad goes to church on the holidays. And because her mom was so religious, and my mom and her mom were really close before her mom died."

"Speaking of religious families," Abbie said, "I heard that Anthony's mom used to go to church every day."

"But I thought Anthony's mom died! That's what everyone always says," said Shamus.

"Well, yeah, she did. I guess one morning Anthony's dad dragged her out of church, took her home, and beat her up so bad that she died. Then they said she fell down the stairs and died, so his dad never went to jail or anything."

"No way!" Shamus shouted. "Where did you hear that?"

"I have my sources," Abbie said, smiling. "Well, okay, if you really want to know, Farley told me." Farley, the school bully, was Shamus's "twin cousin"—their mothers, who were two sisters, married their fathers, who were brothers. Shamus and Farley were born three hours apart, and although you could see quite a bit of resemblance—the bulging blue eyes, the freckles—Shamus's skeptical banter was harmless compared to Farley's cruel mockery of all his peers' flaws. And although the two were family, they didn't get along.

"Guys, it's really not nice to gossip," Sarah said. "And anyway, where is Anthony? I invited him to the party and I never heard anything from him."

"You invited *Anthony*?" Shamus said. "Sarah, what were you thinking? He'd stink up the whole place if he came here. And he looks at you with that dumb look on his face. Has anyone even heard him talk?"

"Oh my gosh, once," Abbie said, "in Mrs. Santi's class, she called on him and he—"

"Be quiet!" Sarah snapped. "Stop talking about Anthony! He might be hurt or in trouble. You guys have no reason to be mean to him," she said harshly. "And anyway, I'm worried about him. I'm going to call him and find out if he's okay."

She picked up the phone on the side table, pulled out a little phone book from the drawer in the table and looked up Anthony's number. "Here it is," she said, dialing the number.

Shamus looked at Basil and rolled his eyes. Basil felt uncomfortable. He agreed with Shamus that Anthony was smelly and weird. But at the same time, he was a human being, after all. Basil felt kind of bad for him.

"Hello? Hello?" Sarah said into the receiver. Then she put the phone back on the hook. "I thought I heard some grunt or something, but then whoever it was hung up. Let me try one more time. Maybe I dialed the wrong number." She dialed again.

"Why bother, Sarah? I mean, unless you're going to prank him. Here, give me the phone," Shamus said. She shot him an angry look and pushed his hand away as he tried to grab the phone from her.

"Hello? Hello? Is Anthony there?" Sarah said again. "Oh. I'm sorry. Well, can you just—Hey! He hung up on me!"

"Who?" Abbie asked.

"Anthony's dad, or whoever that was," Sarah said. "At first, when he picked up, I just heard breathing, and then when I asked if Anthony was there, he said," she imitated the man with a gruff, mean voice, "'He's busy. Don't call back!' And then he hung up before I could even leave a message. I'm really worried, you guys!"

"You're always worried, Sarah," Shamus said. "And I'm sure he's fine. I mean, his dad is crazy, but Anthony's probably crazy too, so they're used to each other."

"Actually, Shamus, Sarah has a point, for once," Christian said, taking an unusually serious tone. "Anthony is weird, I'll say that, but the poor kid probably has issues. It's obvious something is seriously wrong in his life. I kind of feel sorry for him."

"Yeah," Abbie said. "One time Anthony came to school with bruises and cuts all over his face and arms. I think they sent him over to the social worker that day, because after he came into literature class that morning I saw the teacher whisper something to him and then he left the room. Everyone knows his dad beats him up, and I guess we probably shouldn't joke about it. I mean, it is really sad. But my mom said it's one of those things that no one seems to know what to do about. She said she heard from her friend who works at the school that they tried to take him away from his dad a couple of times, but he always came back and said he'd changed, and they gave Anthony back to him. So who knows."

Basil didn't say anything, but the wheels in his mind were turning fast. He'd been sitting next to Sarah when she called Anthony's house. Although he couldn't hear everything, when Anthony's dad said "Don't call back!" he could hear the dad's loud voice crack through the receiver, and it was scary. Suddenly Anthony didn't seem like such a creepy loser, but more like a pathetic, wounded creature, alone with that cruel father of his.

"Well anyway, give me another cookie," Shamus said. "This is depressing. Let's talk about something else." The kids continued to talk, and even Sarah stopped talking about Anthony and tried to talk about other things. They all started discussing the different teachers at St. Norbert's, doing impersonations of the really mean ones.

Basil drifted off, unable to participate in their fun. He felt sick to his stomach thinking about poor Anthony, and how guilty he felt for shunning him all the months he'd been attending St. Norbert's. His mother had always been firm with him: Treat others the way you would want to be treated. Don't judge a book by its cover. Don't judge a man until you've walked a mile in his shoes. She was full of lessons about how to treat others kindly, and he was too cool to care.

And for the first time in his life, Basil was truly ashamed of himself.

⁖⁂⁖

BASIL'S MOM TOLD HIM FIRMLY that she wanted him home no later than nine o'clock, but when Shamus's family picked Basil up from the party and asked him if he wanted to go out for pizza, he couldn't resist. So he insisted that his mom wouldn't mind, and he certainly hoped she wouldn't, even though he knew she would.

An hour later, Basil's stomach started to feel sick when the car pulled down his small gravel driveway and he saw his mom in the doorway waiting for him. She gave a half-hearted smile and wave to the family as they dropped Basil off, and then when they were out of sight she grabbed him forcefully by the arm and dragged him into the house.

"It's ten o'clock at night!" She was fuming. "Where *were* you?" Basil stammered, trying to spit out an answer. "You know what, I don't even want to know where you were. You are *grounded* for the rest of winter break. I want you in your room, doing your homework, and that's it—no fun, no friends, no nothing. And you better not be late again. *E-ver.* Do you hear me?"

"Yeah, but—"

"I don't want to hear any 'buts' from you. You knew you were supposed to be home at nine o'clock, and not only did you come home an hour late, but you didn't even call to ask my permission! I'm so mad I could spit! Go to bed, now!"

Basil ran up to his room, not sure if he should be afraid or extremely mad. Whenever he got into trouble, his mom wouldn't let him say anything. He threw himself onto his bed.

"It's not fair!" he said, smashing his fist into a pillow. "You didn't even let me explain!"

He lay on his bed for a long time, trying to figure out what he would do for two weeks alone in the house.

When he had calmed down a bit, he sat up and looked out the tall window behind his bed. The window faced the backyard with its never-ending expanse of trees. The night was charming in its wintry way—the cold air made the stars seem more sparkly. Basil could see what seemed like every star in the universe hovering above the trees. It was then that Basil noticed something unusual on the skyline in the distance for the first time. It looked like a tiny, tiny cross just slightly above the trees. Basil had an old pair of binoculars that once belonged to his mom. He dug them out of one of his drawers and focused on the cross in the distance. He was fascinated by what he saw—it looked like the shiny dome of a church, with a cross mounted on top, reflecting the moonlight. That meant there was a church somewhere on the other side of the forest, perhaps beyond the wide lake that sat behind their house.

Suddenly Basil forgot all about his fight with his mom; he even forgot about being grounded for all of winter break. Basil could only think of two things now, two new goals. The first was that some time in the near future he *had* to find that church. He wanted to see it up close. It must be very tall or on a big hill to stretch even above the large pine trees, and surely it was in a remote place, as his house was in the middle of nowhere; there wasn't another town for miles.

The second goal—and surely a more noble and important one—was his resolution to befriend pathetic Anthony. Basil could only imagine the kinds of punishments Anthony got from his dad. After all, if his father really had beaten Anthony's mother to death, he could do the same thing to his son. The worst part, to Basil, was that he realized now that he had never, ever been nice to Anthony.

It was at this point that Basil decided he had a new mission in life. When school was back in session in a few weeks, he promised himself, he would go out of his way to treat Anthony better.

January

Chapter 14

WINTER BREAK WAS TOO LONG; it dragged on forever, and Basil's mom was stubborn—she refused to let up on the grounding, even when Shamus called and invited Basil out to dinner with his family twice. So when school started back up, Basil was actually happy, for the first time in his life, to see a vacation from school end.

He was also looking forward to starting on his new mission—being nicer to Anthony. His first chance to do so was in the last class of the day on Monday—Mrs. Santi's Church History class.

Church History was Basil's most boring class, and the kids were always antsy, usually chattering, throwing spitballs, passing notes, and acting crazy. Basil came to class early that day, hoping that if he sat near Anthony, no one would notice. Anthony was always the first kid in class. He had no friends to talk with in the halls between classes, so he got to each class as soon as the one before was over. He always sat in the last seat in the back corner of the right-hand side of the room, right next to the window. Usually he was hunched over his desk drawing something all through class.

When Basil got to class, no one was there but Anthony, who was staring out the window. So Basil went to the right back corner of the room and sat in the chair next to Anthony's. "Hey," he said, putting his books down. He was out of breath after climbing two flights of stairs. Anthony didn't budge. He just continued to stare out the window.

"Hey," Basil said again. Anthony didn't respond.

Basil paused for a minute, considering moving to a different seat. Maybe this kindness thing wasn't worth it. After all, in being nicer to Anthony, he was putting his own reputation at risk. Everyone at school treated Anthony worse than they would treat a dead, decaying rat found in their desk. So naturally anyone caught hanging out with him would be an outcast by association. But Basil's conscience started to nag at him, so he turned once more to Anthony, reached out his hand and gave him a light tap on the shoulder.

"Hey Anthony, what's up?"

Anthony turned to him quickly, almost startled. He didn't say a word. He just looked at Basil with a blank stare, blinked, stared again, then turned toward his notepad and started doodling.

Before Basil could say anything else, a pack of kids entered the room, led by Shamus's cousin Farley. Farley hadn't noticed Basil up to this point, which was a good thing, in Basil's mind. The other *News* staffers had warned him that Farley and his pack were best avoided. They were mostly harmless, physically, but they really enjoyed tearing a person to shreds with merciless teasing. Of course, poor Anthony was a frequent victim of their ridicule.

Farley wasn't the typical ape-like bully, with bulging muscles and a mean look plastered on his face. He was a shortish, wiry kid with freckles, red hair, and a loud voice. He was also exceptionally good at sports, and pretty girls always squealed and giggled when he scored a home run in baseball or a goal in soccer.

But Farley had one of the cruelest hearts a boy his age could possibly have. Even the older kids at school, particularly the ones who had ears a little too large or a nose a little too pointy, too many pimples or a weak build, were afraid of Farley, who showed no mercy. He was also one of the few kids who was always on academic probation at St. Norbert's; most people believed his father, a wealthy contractor who also had a reputation for being a bully, had scared Mr. Fishburn into allowing Farley to stay.

As luck would have it, Farley and his friends sat right next to Basil.

"So anyway, guys, listen to this," Farley said as he sat down. "My little brother is learning how to make fun of people. I'm so proud of him. Oh, hi, Anthony," Farley said quietly as Mrs. Santi and the other kids filed into the room. "I like your dirty uniform.

Hey, when was the last time you washed your uniform, Anthony? Five years ago?"

"More like ten years ago," said Marcus, Farley's best friend, and another person on the academic probation list allowed to stay at St. Norbert's because of his athletic abilities. They both started laughing.

"Anthony, did you remember about our test today?" Farley said. "We're still going to help each other for the test, right?"

"Yeah, you give us the answers, and we'll help you by not beating you up after school," Marcus said. Although Farley was too small to really pick a fight with anyone, Marcus was big enough to beat someone to a bloody pulp.

Strangely, Anthony didn't even flinch. He totally ignored them. Basil secretly hoped and prayed that Farley and Marcus wouldn't notice him and start teasing him, too.

That is, until they took things one step too far. Marcus reached over and pushed the side of Anthony's head. Anthony winced in pain. "Hey, Anthony, did you hear us? We're talking to you. You're going to give us answers to the test, right, freak?"

"If you two had half a brain put together, maybe you could come up with your own answers," Basil said, terrified seconds after the words left his mouth.

Both Farley and Marcus turned their heads away from Anthony and toward Basil in shock. "Shut up, new nerd," Farley said. "Who are you, anyway? Oh, I remember. You're my geek cousin's new best friend."

"Yeah, he's the one who writes the miracle articles for the school paper," Marcus said. Farley opened his mouth to say something, but Mrs. Santi began class, and, to Basil's relief, Marcus and Farley were suddenly too worried about cheating on the test to pay any more attention to Basil and Anthony.

·ঞ·   Chapter 15

THE NEXT DAY IN MRS. SANTI'S CLASS, Basil once again sat near Anthony. Even though he was terrified of Marcus and Farley, he didn't want to give up on his effort to befriend Anthony—especially after seeing firsthand the way he was treated. Once again he said hi to Anthony, and Anthony didn't say a word in return. Basil shrugged it off and told himself he would keep trying until he eventually convinced Anthony that he wasn't going to tease him.

But something terrible happened. It didn't seem so bad at first—Mrs. Santi gave a lecture on early saints of the church, and among them, she talked about St. Basil the Great. Of course, being the way she was, she had to draw attention to the fact that Basil's name was derived from St. Basil the Great, at which point Basil heard Farley and Marcus laugh to themselves. But then the worst thing happened—Mrs. Santi gave the class a group assignment, and as luck would have it, Basil, Anthony, Farley, Marcus, and Christian were placed in a group together.

At first, Farley and Marcus started tearing into Anthony with the same "I like your dirty uniform" line they had used the day before. Christian whispered to Basil that they said this to him every day, and some days, they would even take their pens and scribble little things on his shirt, and then laugh at it the next time they saw him, because he always wore the same shirt and never washed it. But soon Basil started to get irritated.

"Shut *up*! Can't you think of something better to do? Leave him alone," Basil said.

"Oh, look," Farley said. "It's a *miracle*. Basil the Great Geek here to save his best friend Anthony."

"Maybe he's Anthony's guardian angel," Marcus said, laughing.

"Why don't you guys grow up," Christian said. Basil was a little surprised that Christian would stand up for them, since she was usually the one picking on everyone in their *News* friends circle.

"*You* grow up, freak. You're just as weird as Anthony and Basil the Great Geek. I like your thrift-store bag," Farley said to her, pointing to the old army bag she carried with her everywhere.

"For your information, I got this bag from a thrift store *intentionally*. I can afford to shop at designer stores. I just don't want to," she said.

"Whatever, weirdo," Farley said.

"Farley, Christian, I hope you're talking about St. Nicholas of Myra and what he did for the church," Mrs. Santi said.

"We are, Mrs. Santi," Farley said sweetly. Mrs. Santi rolled her eyes behind Farley's back.

"Don't let Farley bother you," Christian whispered to Basil. "I think you did the right thing by sticking up for Anthony."

Basil was glad Christian's nicer side was coming out—he hated it when she was so bratty.

After class, when Farley and Marcus and most of the other kids had left, Anthony reached over silently and tugged on Basil's shirtsleeve. "Thanks," he said, his wide eyes staring at Basil. He said nothing else, quickly turning to leave.

Basil was shocked. Anthony had never spoken to him before, or to anyone at school for that matter. He was a little embarrassed to be associated with Anthony, but at the same time, he felt he had done something good by finally getting through to him.

⠿ Chapter 16

BUT JUST AFTER BASIL HAD GOTTEN THROUGH TO HIM, Anthony disappeared for a few days. Basil began to wonder what had happened to him; none of the other *News* staffers seemed to know.

"Why do you even care?" Shamus said one day at lunch. "The kid's weird, and if you spend too much time with him, it might ruin your reputation. I've already heard from some other kids that you've been talking to him."

"Well, maybe I don't care about my reputation anymore," Basil said, annoyed. "I care about sticking up for a human being who has a really horrible life."

"Sticking up for him—are you crazy? I mean, it's okay to be nice and all, but if you keep talking like that, *you'll* start to get treated the way Anthony does. Just don't say I didn't warn you, man."

The bell rang.

"See you in gym class," Shamus said.

THE FOLLOWING MONDAY, Basil and Shamus were putting on their gym uniforms in the locker room when they heard a bunch of kids laughing a few rows away. Other kids started to move toward the noise, so Basil and Shamus followed.

Basil was horrified to find Anthony standing frozen in front of his locker as Farley, Marcus, and the gang of bullies picked on him. Marcus started pushing him around, and then Farley tugged at his shirt.

"Let's see you take off that shirt," Farley said. "We all know you never take a bath, and you never, ever take off that nasty shirt, do you?" he said.

The other kids were cheering. "Take off the shirt, take off the shirt," they said in unison. Basil was disgusted, but helpless—the crowd of boys was too big to break through. He looked around for their gym teacher, Mr. Adonis, but he was busy in his office working on whatever mysterious paperwork gym teachers work on; he always ignored fights anyway. "Boys will be boys," he would say to Principal Fishburn when asked why he didn't break up fights.

Then it happened. While Farley was tugging on Anthony's shirt, Marcus pushed Anthony so hard that the shirt ripped apart; Anthony fell to the floor, and what remained of his shirt was in Farley's hand.

At that moment, everyone, even Farley, gasped in horror. Skinny, frail Anthony lay on the cold, lime-green floor tiles; he had a gigantic, scabby burn mark on his back. Everyone gaped, then slowly turned and walked away in a flurry of whispers, leaving Anthony alone. It was obvious that the beaten boy was being picked on by a much bigger person at home. For once, the throbbing mob of bullies had mercy.

When the kids had cleared away, Anthony ran to the bathroom, shirtless, and hid in a stall. Basil ran after him. He heard Anthony crying, but he didn't want to embarrass him. So he quietly slid his own shirt under the door of the stall. Basil's mom always made him keep an extra uniform in his locker, in case he spilled something on his clothes or needed it for some other reason. As soon as he pushed the shirt under the door, he heard Anthony stop crying. In fact, Basil heard nothing on the other side of the door. He paused in front of the stall for a second or two, trying to decide if he should say something. Anthony didn't speak, so Basil went back to his locker, finished dressing, and left to play soccer with the rest of the class. He prayed that gym class would end quickly, as the events in the locker room had caused his stomach to feel twisted and gurgly.

❀ Chapter 17

THAT THURSDAY'S NEWSPAPER MEETING was good—it was the deadline day for January, and Basil turned in his article about Fotini's miraculous healing, helped edit other people's articles, and even got to sit next to Christian and edit her story. He dared not admit it to anyone, but he still liked hanging out with her—she was becoming a good friend. After the newspaper meeting, Anthony came up to Basil silently when the room had cleared.

"Hi," he said quietly as Basil was trying to fit one last book into his overstuffed backpack. "What are you doing after the meeting?" He was wearing the shirt Basil had given him—he wore it every day now since his old shirt was ruined.

Basil was certain that was the longest sentence he had ever heard Anthony speak.

"Uh, well, I should go home. My mom would be really mad if I was late."

"Oh," Anthony said, turning to leave.

"Why?"

Anthony turned to him again. "Do you want to come to my house for a while?"

"Uh, yeah, sure, I guess," said Basil. He wanted to go, but he was worried about several things—his mom being mad if he was late, the other kids seeing him walk home with Anthony, and worst of all, the possibility of Anthony's evil dad being home.

"My dad doesn't come home until really late, usually, so you can come see my room."

"Okay," Basil said, feeling a little bit relieved. Before they left, he went to a pay phone and called his mom at work. She was glad that he called, and said it was fine for him to go to Anthony's, as long as he was home by dinner.

"So, where do you live?" Basil asked as they left school and started walking under a gray sky, the frozen air burning their skin.

"I live on the Southeast Side. It's a long walk, but I'm used to it."

"What happened to your bike?" Basil asked, thinking of Anthony's pathetic pink piece of trash. Basil was walking alongside his trusty blue-and-silver bicycle.

"Oh, uh, my dad, well, he kind of broke it."

Basil regretted asking.

The Southeast Side, also known as "the Skids," was the rough part of town, and Basil never walked there alone. Not to mention the fact that he was fairly certain it was at least a mile away from the school. But he didn't want to put up a fuss, so he dug his gloved hands further into his coat pockets and tried to keep up with Anthony as they walked through the cold winter afternoon.

After walking a mile or so, they turned down a long gravel road that led to a ramshackle wooden house hidden behind monstrously overgrown pine shrubs. The paint was peeling and the whole building looked ready to collapse. A rusty mailbox stood open, and the mail was nearly falling out of it. Anthony went up to the box and picked up the bundle of mail, carrying it up to the door, which was unlocked.

"It's really dark in here," Basil said as he reached to turn on the light in the room. He flicked the switch on and nothing happened. It was cold, too. Basil noticed that it was about as cold inside as it was outside.

"We don't have electricity any more," Anthony said. "We lost that when my dad got laid off from his last job. We still have the phone, but I'm pretty sure that will be canceled in the next few days."

"So how do you see at night?" Basil asked. How did he stay warm, Basil wondered.

"I try to go to bed early, and if I need to do homework or something, I use candles. I get them from the dumpster behind the candle shop."

Basil cringed thinking of someone crawling through a

dumpster. Anthony's living situation made Basil feel like a king.

"You mean you get stuff from the garbage?" Basil asked. "Aren't you afraid of rats and diseases and stuff?"

"Not really," said Anthony.

It sounded pretty nasty to Basil. He didn't know what to say, so he changed the subject.

"If your dad doesn't work, where is he now?"

"Well, sometimes he does work—he's a temp, so he works every now and then," Anthony said. "And after he works, he usually goes to Donovan's bar a few blocks away. He hangs out there a lot."

"So who takes care of you, if your dad's always at work or at the bar?"

"I take care of myself mostly," he said. "My dad usually spends all his money at the bar, but sometimes I take some of it while he's passed out from being drunk and use it to buy food and water. Otherwise, I have to eat from the dumpsters."

"You actually *eat* from dumpsters? How can you stand it?" Basil knew it was a rude thing to ask, but the nosey journalist in him had to know.

"It's hard, but you get used to it. And when I can't get used to it, I just pray to God to keep going," Anthony said. Basil was surprised—he had no idea Anthony was that way.

"Wow," Basil said. It was all he could think of.

"This is my room," Anthony said, pushing open a door that was barely hanging on its hinges, as if it had been busted open more than a few times. The room was a complete mess—Basil's mother never would have tolerated a mess half the size of this. The entire floor was covered with papers and odds and ends, and the walls were covered with all sorts of paintings and drawings. There was no furniture—not even a bed. Anthony slept on a pile of dirty blankets in the corner of the room. Next to the "bed" was a cardboard box turned upside down, with several candles of all shapes and sizes on it. Anthony picked up a matchbook off the floor and lit all the candles. The room was still dark, but now had a warm

glow that made Basil feel a little more comfortable. It was then that he noticed a small gray rabbit sitting in the corner opposite the bed, munching on an old math worksheet.

"This is my pet bunny, Mario," he said. "I found him on the

side of the road one day. He had been hit by a car, but only his back leg was broken. So I took him home and helped him get better, and now he stays by me. He even sleeps with me at night."

"Cool," Basil said. He tried to pick Mario up, but the rabbit ran to the other side of the room and hid under a stack of empty boxes.

Basil looked around the walls at all the drawings—of animals, airplanes, nature scenes, and even a few icons like the ones at Holy Resurrection.

"Did you do all these drawings?" he asked.

"Yeah," Anthony said. "Once, I found a huge art kit with some pieces missing in a dumpster behind an art store, and I brought it home and started drawing."

"So are you into icons?"

"Can you keep a secret?"

Basil hadn't planned on telling anyone he'd been with Anthony, let alone that he had seen his room.

"Sure," he said.

"Well, my uncle sometimes drops by here at night and leaves things on my window sill. Sometimes he leaves money and food. Sometimes he brings me little gifts, like books and icons. Once he left a huge book of icons—it had all sorts of paintings in it, and directions on how to paint your own, because he knows I like to draw. I don't have paint, so I just use crayons and colored pencils, mostly. My uncle's an artist, you know—like me. But you can't tell anyone about any of this, please, Basil. If my dad ever found out about my uncle coming here to give me things . . ."

Basil didn't know what to say. Before going to Anthony's house, he'd thought his own life was difficult. But after seeing the way Anthony lived, he realized his life was easy by comparison. He paused for a moment, and when Anthony didn't say anything, he decided to ask the burning question on his mind, even if it was a pretty brash thing to ask.

"So what would happen—I mean, if your dad found out about your uncle?"

"Did you see that big burn on my back?"

"Uh, yeah," Basil said. "It was kinda hard to miss."

"He'd do worse than that to me if he knew my uncle was coming here to give me things."

Basil tried to imagine what could be worse than that burn. "What would he do to you?" As soon as he said it, he knew he shouldn't have.

Anthony paused for a moment. "I don't really want to say. He's sick. I just try to forgive him, and pray that he'll change." Anthony crouched down to sweep away some of the mess off a spot on his floor, then sat down. Basil wasn't sure what do to, so he moved an old cardboard box full of used-up candles and sat down as well.

"Can't someone help you? Why can't your uncle come and take you away?"

"When I was little, my uncle, my mom's brother, used to come over here all the time. But then one day, my dad went crazy on him and told him never to come back. My dad is a sick man. He has some kind of mental disease. He's nice sometimes and other times . . . even when he's sober he can be brutal." Basil looked over his shoulder. He was starting to worry that Anthony's dad would return home.

"One day he blew up and said he would kill my uncle," Anthony continued. "He started punching him when he was visiting. So my uncle never came back—well, my dad doesn't know that he still comes. And anyway, it wouldn't be right for my uncle to take me—it's not the right time yet. But I keep praying that when the time comes, it'll happen." Anthony seemed to explode to life, as if all that time he sat quietly in school not uttering a single word to anyone he was holding a tremendous amount inside of him that he suddenly felt comfortable revealing to Basil. Basil was stunned that Anthony would tell an almost perfect stranger such intimate, secret things about himself. He wondered if he was the first person to ever hear such things about Anthony's life.

"I hope it happens soon," Basil said, feeling very angry at Anthony's father. "How can you forgive your dad?"

"I guess I just try to remember that he doesn't know what he's doing when he hurts me."

Anthony paused for a long time. "I know my life is hard," he continued. "People don't like me at school. I sometimes wonder if *anyone* likes me, other than my uncle—but that doesn't matter, because God made me for a reason, and I have to live my life knowing that God's love is better than anything else."

Basil wondered how he could be so optimistic.

"God has answered prayers. He protects me. And he even answered one of my biggest prayers."

"What's that?" Basil asked.

"My prayer for a friend."

Basil looked away, feeling embarrassed. After a moment he looked up and saw tears in Anthony's eyes. Basil suddenly felt awkward at the burden of having a friend like Anthony; and yet, he was very, very glad that he'd decided to help him.

Just then, they heard a door slam—Anthony's father had entered the house, and he sounded drunk. "Anthony!" he screamed. Basil was terrified.

"Here," Anthony said. He turned and whispered to Basil. "Let me help you climb out the window. Then run. There is a trail that goes through the forest. Get your bike and take that trail to the highway. You should be able to find your way from there."

"Come with me," Basil begged Anthony. "I'm sure my mom wouldn't mind if you stayed at our house. There's plenty of room."

"No," Anthony said, shaking his head. "It's not time yet."

February

✿ Chapter 18

FEBRUARY WAS ALWAYS A HARD MONTH FOR BASIL. Usually school was getting harder and more dull by the day, the weather was nasty, the teachers were more irritable, the kids were always passing around miserable colds and flus, and his mom was angrier—she hated Valentine's Day, which reminded her of her loneliness. As for Basil, Valentine's Day meant nothing to him—but at St. Norbert's, for the February issue, they always allowed the students to place little "love ads," "shout-outs" to their girlfriends or boyfriends, in the paper. Basil wasn't sure if he should use the opportunity to place an anonymous ad to Christian—but he decided not to. He had no guts, and having never had a girlfriend, he was terrified that if she found out he liked her, it would get awkward and uncomfortable between them. And he ended up getting a horrible flu anyway, so he missed school for the first half of the week of Valentine's Day.

Basil was so distracted by the February blahs that he almost forgot to start working on his next column, which was due the following Thursday. That weekend in church, Doctor Raphael mentioned to Basil that he had told his son about Basil's articles, and that his son, who was a missionary working at an orphanage in Mongolia, had agreed to send Basil a letter about a miracle he'd experienced.

That week, Basil anxiously looked in his mail on Monday and Tuesday. Nothing. He had to get the article before Thursday—he was running out of time before the deadline. Finally, on Wednesday, he found a thick envelope covered with foreign stamps lying on the countertop when he got home from school. The letter inside wasn't typed, but the handwriting was legible. He sat down on a couch with a bottle of purple pop and read the letter to himself:

Dear Basil,

My name is Mousa Raphael and I am the son of Doctor Raphael, the man you met in church. My dad told me about your wonderful column for your school newspaper, and I am very inspired by what you are doing. Since you are writing about miracles, I thought I would share with you a miracle I experienced myself.

A few years ago, when I had been fighting with my father and causing much pain in his life, he suggested that I go on a service trip to another country. I had some experience in construction, so a particular organization sent me to work on a site high up on a cliff that was going to be a library for the villagers. One hot morning, my job was to begin excavations with a few other workers. I drove the bulldozer.

I remember in the heat I started feeling dizzy and sweaty as I put the gears in motion to start breaking ground. Not a moment after I began to dig, the bulldozer screeched to a halt; I had hit something rock-hard that wasn't going to budge. I started to feel nauseous as I tried again—the same thing. Only this time, the bulldozer actually jolted backwards a bit when it hit the ground. I inched the machine back into place and tried a third time. This time the dozer scraped a little harder and then suddenly it began rolling backwards. Realizing that there wasn't far for it to go before it rolled right off the cliff, I leapt out of the dozer and it pitched over the side, dashed to pieces on the rocks below.

I was shaken, and I got a concussion from the fall. My coworkers took me to a nearby hospital, where I lay for a day or two. While I was recovering, some other volunteers returned to the site with shovels and began digging by hand, so as not to lose another expensive bulldozer. Strangely, there was no large rock preventing them from digging. The soil, to everyone's shock, was loose and unusually easy to dig through.

Everyone had theories about the cause of the bulldozer's fall. Some said the machine was flawed. Others said it was old and probably malfunctioned after too many years of use. One person, who didn't like me very much, said I had been drinking beforehand! I was feeling a little sick to my stomach that day, but I can assure you that I hadn't touched alcohol that morning.

When they got down ten feet, though, all their theories fell apart. What they found was one of the great discoveries of this century: human bones that turned out to be the wonder-working relics of three saints who had died 500 years ago!

At first, no one was sure what to do with the relics. Local priests came and with the help of experts carefully removed all the remains and brought them to a nearby monastery. Soon it was revealed that a number of people in the area had been having dreams and visions about these saints for many years. Apparently the saints appeared to different folks in town and told them about their martyrdom and about the location of their remains. One well-known monk said these saints—a priest, a layman, and a young girl—had been brutally martyred, killed at the site of what was once their church by their enemies. Many did not fully believe at first, despite the visions, that the relics were those of saints. How could we know that a bunch of old bones buried under the earth were saints' relics? But then the healings started happening. Many people were actually healed when cloths rubbed on the bones were touched to their skin. A local historian did some research and discovered that indeed, there was once a church at the site of the excavation, and it was burned by the villagers' enemies, about 500 years ago.

The experience changed me deeply. Until that experience falling off the bulldozer, my soul was very sick. I was a very angry person. I had no faith. I hated most people, and only used them to get what I wanted out of life. I enjoyed drinking until it started wearing me down. My father and I were constantly at odds. I had no direction in my life, no job, no sense of purpose. I worshipped only myself—until I realized the moment I fell out of that bulldozer, coming within inches of falling to my death over the cliff, how weak and pathetic I really was—hardly worth worshipping. There had to be something beyond this life, I thought as I lay in that hospital bed.

God saved me by bringing me to these saints. Our miraculous find restored my faith and made a believer out of me. And this was only the beginning. Since finding these saints, my life has been transformed. I am now a full-time missionary overseas and studying to be a priest. My specialty is still construction; so as soon as this sacred site was revealed, we were commissioned to restore the church that had once existed 500 years ago in honor of the three martyrs. I applaud what you are doing and am so enthusiastic about it that I will lead you to yet another person who has experienced a real miracle. I know a builder who experienced a miraculous healing of a brain tumor through a monk of the Holy Mountain. Ask my dad or Father Maximos to tell you more about the Holy Mountain. The builder's name is Yousef Ammar; Father Maximos will know how to contact him. Please send Father Maximos my regards.

Yours in Christ,
Mousa Raphael

Chapter 19

"So, Father, what are relics?" Basil asked old Father Maximos as they sat in the church office the following Sunday after Liturgy. Basil had been going to church on and off, mostly when his mom had time to drive him if she planned on going in to work for the morning to do some overtime.

"Relics? Relics are the remains of saints—sometimes their bodies, bones, or even their clothes and other possessions. Whenever the relics of a holy person are found, we revere and preserve them. Often relics are used to heal people."

"Have you ever seen a relic, Father?" Basil asked.

"Have I seen a relic? Of course! I have seen relics of all kinds. Our church here has a relic right inside the altar."

"Really? Can I see it?"

"Oh, no, I'm afraid not, Basil," Father Maximos laughed. "Our relics, a few small bones of a child martyr from the tenth century, are sealed inside the altar table."

Shoot, Basil thought to himself.

"Sometimes," Father Maximos continued, "whole bodies are found that have not decomposed, even though the saints have been dead for centuries."

Basil thought of *Resurrected Corpses*, a movie he had seen recently about the dead coming out of their graves, their dirty gray skin dripping off and their eyeballs falling out as they went around town killing people.

"Not decomposed? Doctor Raphael's son said something about finding saints' bodies, but I thought he was just talking about finding their bones or something. How does that happen?" Father saw the horror in Basil's eyes and tried to explain.

"Sometimes it is just bones," Father said. "Other times, though, holy people are found incorrupt—their bodies are still whole. They still have skin on them. They usually smell strongly the same way the weeping icon at our church does—a beautiful smell. It may sound frightening, but I assure you that they look quite serene—at peace. Not like monsters. Such people often have a sort of holy glow to them. And they are very much alive—perhaps not in the way that you and I are, but alive with God in His heavenly kingdom."

Basil watched Father Maximos's hands move about as he spoke. He was very lively for such an old man.

"You know what, I'll tell you an interesting story," Father Maximos went on. "There is a saint on an island far away whose body did not decompose. It lies in a tomb inside a monastery. This saint actually gets out of his tomb a few times a year and walks around, visiting people in need."

"No *way!*" Basil said, his eyes bulging out of his head in disbelief.

"Yes way!" Father Maximos chuckled. "The slippers he wears become worn out, sandy and dirty. They are covered with seaweed from walking on the beach of the island. That's how they know that the villagers' stories of his visits are true. The interesting thing is that sometimes the monks at the monastery can't open his tomb. It is said that when this happens, he is not really there, but that is when he is walking about helping people."

"Come on, Father Maximos. Seriously? There's no way that can be real."

"Would *I* make that up? I have changed his dirty shoes myself when I was a young priest, visiting the monastery where they keep him."

"Really?"

"Yes, really," he said with a smile.

"So, what does it mean when that happens, like, when they find a body that hasn't rotted away?"

"No one knows for sure, as with most miracles," Father

Maximos said. "But as I said before, we are pretty sure that when we find a body of a Christian that hasn't rotted after many years, we know that person was holy."

Basil paused, thinking over everything in his mind.

"Now if you'll excuse me, I must get back to the coffee hour and those delicious donuts that Fotini brought. An old man needs his nourishment! God bless you, my boy."

⁖

"So anyway, after he got out of the hospital they told him that the reason the bulldozer couldn't dig was because there were three long-lost saints buried ten feet below the surface." Basil told the *News* kids about Mousa Raphael's letter during lunch on Monday.

"What happened after that?" Shamus asked. For a self-proclaimed "skeptical journalist," Shamus was unusually interested, even *excited*, about hearing the rest of the story.

"Let me guess," Christian butted in, the sarcastic ring in her voice making everyone groan in annoyance. "He suddenly decided he believed in Jesus and lived happily ever after?" No one was amused.

"Well, yeah," Basil said. Christian raised her hands in a way that said, "See what I mean?"

"I think if you saw something miraculous like that, you might think twice about your beliefs, too, Christian," Sarah said.

"So, anyway," Basil said, trying to steer away from a tense moment, "what I did was I wrote about how I got this letter from this stranger in another country, and then I told Mr. Dixon to print the whole letter as it is."

"Good idea," Shamus said.

"Hey, not to change the subject," said Basil, "but where has Anthony been lately?"

"I don't know what the deal is with that kid," Christian said. "There are all sorts of rumors going around school about what

95

happened to him. Some kids say they heard he was in the hospital, and others say his dad beat him up really bad. Some people even think he ran away. Poor kid."

Basil had a feeling it was most likely that his father had somehow hurt him. He wished there was some way he could help, but he was too afraid to go to Anthony's house to check up on him.

March

FINALLY, MARCH CAME ROARING IN. Basil had managed to turn in a story a month since September, and he only had three more stories to write for the rest of the school year—one each for March, April, and May. He didn't want to procrastinate on the next articles—he knew that if he let time slip by, as he had in February, he would get himself in trouble. His math grades were terrible again. He was certain he would be getting a bad progress report in the mail, and undoubtedly his mom would be mad.

So it was imperative that he get his March article out of the way before the deadline got any closer. He was pretty sure that his next story would be an interview with Yousef Ammar, the man Mousa Raphael mentioned in his letter, who was healed of a brain tumor. He couldn't interview Mr. Ammar face-to-face, but Father Maximos gave Basil the man's phone number. He planned on calling him soon.

BASIL *HATED* USING THE PHONE; his mother always joked that she was "phone phobic," and she had apparently passed this trait on to him—not a good thing for a would-be journalist. He procrastinated all through March, even though he'd promised himself he wouldn't, finding excuses not to call Mr. Ammar. Finally, his deadline was a week away; he *had* to call him. He had no excuses; his mom had even approved of the call, considering that Mr. Dixon gave Basil a special allowance to cover the long distance charges. His stomach started churning as he approached the phone and began dialing, terrified that in his nervousness he would forget all his questions and sound like a fool. The phone rang twice; a man with a very thick accent answered with what sounded like "hello."

"Hi, is Mr. Ammar there?"

"Who there?"

"This is Basil, I'm a writer for the . . ."

"No want any, stop calling here!" the man shouted.

Basil held the receiver up to his ear, partly in shock that someone had hung up on him. But then he realized that the man probably thought he was trying to sell him something. He decided he would try the number one more time.

"Hello?"

"Mr. Ammar? I just called—I'm not selling anything, Mr. Ammar, please don't hang up." Basil tried to get the words out as quickly as possible in case Mr. Ammar hung up again. "Mousa Raphael told me to call you. My name is Basil and I'm working on an article about miracles for my school paper."

"Mousa? Ah, okay. I know Mousa. Mousa is good boy." Suddenly his tone changed—he sounded like a very nice person. "We work together on many projects. You say you name Basil? Okay, Basil, you tell me what you need."

"Well, I'm writing about miracles, and Mousa said you had a brain tumor that got healed, and I was wondering if you could tell me about that, like, what happened?"

"Okay, okay, I see. Do you have pencil ready and paper? I know you reporters take long notes. It's a long story and I don't want you miss anything."

"Yes, I'm ready."

"Okay. See, I own construction company—I design and build houses, businesses, churches. Many years ago I had bad headaches, so I went to doctor and they tell me I had big brain tumor. Terrible, just terrible news for me. But worse, the day after I found out about tumor, I was very angry and upset, and while driving to work I got into terrible, terrible car accident, which cause brain damage. Damage was to part of brain that makes me to laugh and smile. I also suffer memory loss. Few weeks later, I had brain surgery for tumor. *But,* doctor could only remove part of tumor, because of new damage from accident."

Basil was trying to keep up with Mr. Ammar's broken English.

"Next year, I became Christian, started believing in Jesus, and was invited by priest and family to make pilgrimage to holy places. One day we were walking to small monastery on Holy Mountain—this is place where many, many monks live—and a little, little monk came up to us, speaking in different language—not my own or English—to our priest. Suddenly the monk turned to me, put fingers on my head, and before I could say 'no' he started rubbing my temples, speaking or maybe praying in his language. After about fifteen minutes I ask my priest what monk saying. '*Theotokos* loves you,' my priest replied. I don't know if you know what means, this '*Theotokos*'—you Christian?"

Basil was confused. He stammered, unsure if this was a part of the story or if Mr. Ammar was asking him directly.

"I say boy, you a Christian? You believing in Jesus?"

"Well, I'm, uh, not really . . ." before Basil could really figure out how to answer, Mr. Ammar went on.

"*Theotokos* mean God-bearer—it name for Mary, mother of Jesus. We call God-bearer because she bore God in womb when pregnant with Jesus. So, I said to priest, 'This all he says? He has been talking for very long time.' I remember my priest said, 'He's little repetitious.' Finally little monk left us and we went on. I did notice even though we walk uphill, I was not short of breath as I had been for long while—caused by car accident—however, I thought nothing. Later that day, my son, who travel with us, says, 'Hey dad, you told joke!' which was something I had not been able to do since that part of my brain damaged. Again, I didn't think it was very big deal. When I arrived home few days later, I had brain scan at hospital and doctors told me, no more brain tumor, no more brain damage! I was amazed—not just because my health was back, but also because to me, miracle was revealed."

"Wow," Basil said.

"Yes, wow, heh," Mr. Ammar laughed. "I was so happy that I vowed to go back and find little monk who healed me by grace of God. Next summer, I go back to Holy Mountain. I found monastery monk was from, and I ask abbot—that's monk who is like boss of all other monks—I ask him what could I do to thank monk for being healed. The abbot says another monk, named Elder Panteleimon, also visiting Holy Mountain from our country and we could ask him. Elder Panteleimon was told in vision to start monastery in our country, so asked if we could help him build it. It was coincidence that I am contractor and builder—I told this and promised that as soon as I get home, I would build him monastery. That was long time ago. Now, I have built Elder Panteleimon fifteen monasteries, and one under construction now. They are all over this country."

"Wow," Basil said.

"So how do you know Mousa Raphael?" Mr. Ammar asked.

"Well, actually, I don't know Mousa, but I know his dad," Basil said.

"Do you go to Doctor Raphael's church?"

"Yeah, I guess," Basil said.

"What you mean, *I guess*?! Either you *do* or you *don't*."

"I do go. With Father Maximos."

"Ah, yes, Father Maximos, I know him well, for long time. Lovely priest. I built monastery several years ago quite near that church, I think—about five miles away, just outside of that city, what called? Middle Town?"

"Mittleton."

"Yes, yes, Mittleton. Anyway, is lovely city, and lovely church." Basil heard Mr. Ammar cover the phone for a second, and he heard muted yelling in another language. Then Mr. Ammar uncovered the phone. "Excuse me," he said, "business calls. I must go. Did I answer all questions, young reporter?"

"Yes, and thank you so much, Mr. Ammar."

"You welcome. God bless you and you article."

Basil hung up the phone. He went to the cupboard to get a

snack, and as he began opening a creamy oatmeal tart, he froze.

"Wait—did he say there was a monastery near Mittleton?" Basil said aloud, to himself. "That can't be. I've never heard of a—whoa!"

Basil ran up to his bedroom, grabbed his binoculars in a flash and, in the light of the day, scanned the skyline for that small gold cross peeking over the treetops. Finally he spotted it. "That's it!" he shouted, even though he was alone. "That must be the monastery Mr. Ammar built!" Of course, this was even more of an incentive for Basil to hike over there as soon as possible. He just had to find a time to sneak away when his mom wouldn't notice him gone. His only fear (aside from his mother's wrath if she discovered his plans) was getting lost in the dense forest that stood between him and the monastery. "I'll figure it out," he said to himself, hoping deep down that he really would.

❧ **Chapter 21**

THE FOLLOWING MONDAY Anthony returned to school. In Mrs. Santi's class that day, he didn't say a word to anyone; he seemed to slump a little lower in his chair, and even sitting close to him, Basil could barely hear him breathe. Basil tried to make eye contact a few times, to say hi. It was almost as if Anthony wasn't even conscious.

"If you look at him from a certain angle under the fluorescent light in here," Christian whispered to Basil in class, "you can almost see a fading bruise under his eye."

"That's *not* good," Basil said. He didn't want to even imagine what had kept Anthony from coming to school. The truth was, Basil was afraid to ask, and even more afraid to find out.

Fortunately, Farley was absent that day; Basil dreaded seeing Farley, and he found their encounters to be much more painful when Anthony was present.

After class, Anthony came up behind Basil and tapped him on the shoulder.

"Hi," he said, his voice a little scratchy. "How are you?"

Basil wanted to grab him and scream, "*Where have you been?*" but of course he didn't. Instead he said quietly, "I'm okay." He didn't even want to ask Anthony how he was doing. He didn't want to know.

"Do you want to come over today?" Anthony said, much to Basil's shock.

"Oh, well—" he paused and thought for a moment. If he went to Anthony's, he chanced seeing his dad; on the other hand, he was desperate to help Anthony, and any extra time spent with him might give him more chances to persuade Anthony to come live with Basil and his mom.

"Okay," Basil said. "Sure."

Basil unlocked his bike from the main rack and started walking it toward Anthony's house. When they had been walking for a few minutes and the school was no longer in sight, Basil finally got the courage to break the silence with a question.

"Do you think your dad will be home?"

Anthony, seeming to understand Basil's fear, said, "Don't worry, Basil. I thought we could go to my secret place, if that's okay with you. It's an old farmhouse I like to spend time in." It was an unseasonably warm March afternoon, and Basil would prefer exploring an old farmhouse hands down over hanging out at Anthony's dark, creepy shack.

After a long walk, they turned off the road just before it reached Anthony's house. They entered the forest and, due to the thickness of the branches, Basil decided to leave his bike behind. Anthony led him for quite a while through dense forest just beginning to bud in the early spring. Finally they reached a clearing— the forest opened up into a farm pasture. In the middle of the pasture was a large, collapsed barn; several paces away from that was a very old, deserted farmhouse. The house had big holes where there were once windows; the front door was missing. An entire wall in the back of the house had collapsed, opening right up into the outside. There was no furniture in the house, although there were scraps of garbage and other junky items here and there, most likely leftovers from wanderers long gone.

Anthony led Basil to the living room, where his skinny fingers wedged open a loose floorboard near the empty, dark fireplace. Underneath the floorboard were Anthony's hidden treasures, which he was about to show Basil. They sat down on the dusty floor and Anthony began explaining his things.

"This is my most special stuff," Anthony said to Basil, his large eyes looking at him like a little kid sharing some worthless gem with a confidant. "Here, see for yourself—you're my friend—I trust you."

Basil looked through the items as Anthony explained.

"This is where I come when things get really bad with my dad," he said. "He has no idea I come here. He gets mad at me when I'm gone for too long, though, so I can't come here too often."

Among Anthony's treasures were a few small icons and books. Basil also saw a gold cross with tiny designs of Jesus and the apostles etched into it.

"That's my mother's cross necklace," Anthony said as Basil examined it. "I would never wear it, but I wish I could. If my dad ever caught me wearing it, I don't know what he'd do to me."

Basil thought this was a good chance to ask him again to leave his dad. "So, I was thinking, are you sure you don't want to come and live with me and my mom? We have tons of room, and it would be so nice for you there—I'm sure my mom won't—"

"No—no, thank you."

Anthony reached into the hole in the floor and pulled out a crinkled, dirty envelope. "This is my mother's will," he said. "She snuck it to me one day after my dad had hurt her. I think she was worried that one day he might kill her, so she gave it to me to hide. She said my uncle had a copy of it, but that no one else knew about it." Anthony put it back under the floor, hidden from view. They were both quiet for a minute. Basil stared down at Anthony's mother's cross. He felt a strange new appreciation for his own nagging mother, who, despite her sometimes irritating ways, was pretty good to him. He also found himself feeling very angry at Anthony for not doing anything about his dreadful situation.

"Why don't you just leave!" Basil blurted out suddenly, unable to stop the words from coming out of his mouth. Anthony drew back, looking shocked. Then he started to cry. Tears rolled down his face in the most horrible way.

"You don't understand," he said. "You *can't* understand. I know my dad seems like a monster, but I keep hoping and praying he'll change. With enough prayers, many people have changed their ways. I know my dad is really just confused. He feels guilty. He has a picture of my mom next to his mattress, and almost every night when he's drunk he screams and cries in his sleep about how he murdered my mom and about how he didn't mean to do it. It's the demons that make him so crazy, that encourage him to do such things. I know because I've seen them. And my dad is too weak right now to resist."

Demons. Basil felt sick to his stomach.

"My dad has a horrible disease," Anthony said. "But I would be just as bad if I couldn't forgive him. I have seen him be really nice when he's sober, and he tries to change, but then his weakness pulls him back to that bar every night, and when he gets drunk, he has totally given the demons control over him. But my uncle and I keep praying for him, and one day, I believe something will have to change—God will save him."

Basil couldn't bear to see Anthony cry in front of him.

Anthony wiped the tears off his face with his dirty shirt sleeve. After that, it was quiet for several minutes, the two boys sitting in silence. Strangely, it wasn't awkward, as it might have been with others—with Anthony, one came to find a sort of peace in not talking. The sun came out from behind the clouds and Anthony and Basil sat and watched the late afternoon shadows move across the tall grasses, birds chirping happily in celebration of a new spring. A squirrel cautiously crept close to the two boys, but then got scared when Basil moved and scrambled away.

"If you sit still for a long time, the animals start to trust you," Anthony said. "I've had birds come and sit on me before. Sometimes I come here to draw and I'll have squirrels sitting nearby watching—it's nice when they do that, because when they sit near me I can draw them better." Anthony pulled out a sketchpad from the hole in the floor and showed it to Basil. Inside were some of the most realistic drawings Basil had ever seen.

"This is amazing," Basil said.

"Wow, thanks," Anthony said. "That's a real compliment, coming from a person like you. I wish I could draw as well as you can write."

"What do you mean? Your drawing is ten times better than my writing!"

They were both quiet. The squirrel hopped away, chasing after another squirrel that had invaded its territory. Basil had never met anyone like Anthony before. He thought at that moment what an idiot he was, cursing and hating his own father for abandoning him as a baby, when Anthony's father abused him and Anthony still loved him and forgave him.

"By the way," Basil said after a few minutes, "this might seem like a weird question, but how do you afford to go to a private school like St. Norbert's?"

"My dad thinks I go to a public school. He's too drunk to know the difference, anyway, and my uncle secretly pays for school. I like going to St. Norbert's—it's not too bad."

The sun was going down, and Basil started to get nervous about getting home in time for dinner. "I'm sorry, but I have to go home now," he said. He *was* sorry—he felt sick at the thought of leaving poor Anthony alone to face that horrible house of his with no one to protect him.

"Thanks for coming here. I'm really glad you got to hang out for a little bit. You can come back here anytime, if you want."

"Maybe I will," Basil said, feeling rushed. "Thanks, Anthony. I'll see you in school."

"Yeah, see you."

Basil made his way back through the forest to the spot where he had left his bike, maneuvered the bike out of the trees, and rode home as fast as he could.

A FEW DAYS LATER, ANTHONY WAS NOT IN SCHOOL. But the attention of the *News* staffers that day at lunch was on Basil's latest article, on the story of Mr. Ammar's healing—Basil was gaining a reputation at St. Norbert's for his articles.

"They're just cool stories," Christian said, commenting on the articles' success. "I think that's why people like it. You don't have to be religious to enjoy a good story—especially the bulldozer story. That's my favorite."

"I thought you said it was predictable," Shamus said.

"Well, maybe the conversion part, I guess. But how often do you hear about bulldozers falling off cliffs?"

"True," Shamus said.

"I just think it's crazy that these kinds of things like what happened to Mr. Ammar, with that little monk healing him, and that bulldozer guy—it's crazy to think that really happened," Sarah said.

Just then, Scott, the *News* staff's computer whiz, came up to Basil. He looked excited, so surely he didn't notice that he had a big smudge of catsup on his white T-shirt.

"Hey, Basil, great story. Listen, my little sister Beth, your quote-unquote 'secret admirer,'" he said, making large quote symbols with his fingers, "wanted me to give you this. She loves you." Basil took the sticker-decorated love letter and crammed it into his pocket. Beth, Scott's nine-year-old sister, had developed a frighteningly large crush on Basil, which grew with each article he published.

Christian rolled her eyes.

"Tell her I said thanks," Basil said, half-distracted. Even though no one else seemed to notice, Basil was very disturbed that Anthony was gone. This was his third day in a row out of school.

April

ꙮ Chapter 22

APRIL FINALLY CAME, with its milder, warmer weather and visions of summer vacation on the horizon. Basil had seen his article on Mr. Ammar's healing come out a week earlier, the last week of March, and everyone loved it. Even Principal Fishburn wrote a letter to the editor praising Basil's work for the paper—this was great, except that the other kids were starting to get a little jealous of the attention Basil was getting. So Mr. Dixon gave them a pep talk at the first *News* meeting in April, telling all the staffers that their contributions were valued and that just being a part of the staff was a special privilege, since he was highly selective in whom he chose to work on the *St. Norbert News*.

Unfortunately, Anthony was not at that meeting to hear Mr. Dixon's praise of the staff's work. Since Basil had last seen Anthony in that abandoned farmhouse, he had missed nine days of school. In that length of time Basil had three major tests and two papers; he spent much of his time studying or fretting over studying or procrastinating. At a few points he even decided to do a deep cleaning of his bedroom to avoid studying. But always in the back of his mind there sat a shadowy memory of Anthony, and a nagging fear about what might be happening to him.

Finally, two full school weeks had gone by, and not a word had been heard from Anthony. In Mrs. Santi's class that Friday, Christian brought up the fact that he was still absent.

"Hey Basil, where has Anthony been?" Christian whispered. Basil always managed to sit next to Christian in class.

"I don't know—I'm kinda wondering if he's okay."

"Well, what should we do? I mean, is there anything we *can* do? To help him, I mean?" Christian said.

Basil had turned the idea of going to Anthony's house over and over in his mind for days. He hadn't told anyone, because he was afraid that talking about his idea would make it more real; someone was bound to urge him to do it, and the truth was, he didn't want to be the one to have to go over there. But he couldn't help himself; and besides, he figured Christian was just the person he could confess his idea to without being pressured to follow through.

"I guess someone could go to his house and see if he's okay," Basil whispered to her while Mrs. Santi droned on about the eleventh-century schism of the Church.

"Let's go!" Christian whispered excitedly, suddenly energized as she seized hold of his half-hearted suggestion. "My mom and step-dad are leaving tonight for a conference, and my grandma will be watching me, but she really doesn't care what I do as long as I'm home before she goes to bed. We can go over to his house tomorrow!"

Mrs. Santi overheard Christian and stopped in her lecture. "Excuse me, Christian. Did you have something to add about the reasons for the Great Schism?"

Just then, Priscilla, the teacher's pet, starting waving her hand furiously in the front row, distracting Mrs. Santi from her enquiry into Christian's thoughts on a subject she was clueless about, mostly from not paying attention in class. Christian turned again to Basil, waiting for his response.

"Sure," he said. "Yeah, my mom actually will be working tomorrow."

"Great!" she said, showing a surprising amount of enthusiasm. "Can you bike over to my house tomorrow around one in the afternoon? Then you can show me where he lives." Christian scribbled a small map of the town, with an "X" where her house was, and handed it to Basil just before the final bell of the day rang.

⚛ Chapter 23

BASIL HAD NEVER RIDDEN HIS BIKE in a subdivision like Birch Lakes before; in fact, he felt like he was trespassing just riding his less-than-stellar bike down these neatly paved, winding roads leading to house after magnificently rich house. Christian's house was wide and deep, standing majestically beside tall trees, with giant windows and gigantic ceilings, and large, framed photographs of vivid nature scenes covering white walls. The house felt like a giant lodge, with a sunny, stone-floored kitchen, a grand living room with a large, *real* tree, a little bubbling waterfall that ran into a small goldfish pond cut into the hardwood floor, bear rugs, and a huge fireplace with a monstrous moose head over it.

"My parents didn't kill it, of course. We're vegetarians," Christian said as she gave Basil a tour of the house. "My step-grandfather bought it at an auction a few years before he died."

Basil had butterflies in his stomach all morning about going to Christian's house for the first time, without Shamus or anyone else going with him. He had never been friends with a girl before—not since preschool anyway.

"Do you want to see my butterfly collection?"

"Sure, I guess," Basil said, not thrilled about looking at a bunch of dead butterflies pinned to Styrofoam when they had more important things to do. Christian led him through the main hallway and opened a door into a spacious room with several potted trees growing all the way to the high ceiling, and a wall full of wide windows. The sparsely decorated room was filled with colorful butterflies fluttering around from one tree to another, or resting on the petals of one of the many potted flowers in the room.

"This is really my room," she said. "I know what you're thinking.

Butterflies are a little girlie. I try not to be too girlie," she said. "But I just love them. They're so delicate and beautiful. They're the only thing in this world that doesn't disappoint me—ever," she said. Basil was more surprised that Christian's butterflies were *alive*; but he was also a bit surprised that Christian liked butterflies, not because he thought they were girlie; more because he didn't think Christian liked much of *anything*.

Christian pointed out a few of her favorite varieties of butterflies and explained a little bit of the science behind raising them—breeding them and encouraging their growth through the special placement of plants and whatnot.

"I spend hours and hours in this room. I have my own bedroom, but honestly, I just feel much more at home in this room. When my parents are out of town, I usually bring some blankets in here and sleep with my babies," she said. Basil was surprised that Christian could call something her "baby" in seriousness. "My favorite thing is when they come and rest on me. Sometimes I think they're the only things that genuinely *like* me."

"*I* like you, Christian," Basil said, regretting it a moment later. He felt like kicking himself. Why did I say that? he thought to himself.

Christian's face turned red. She looked away awkwardly.

"Yeah, well anyway, let's go tell my grandma we're leaving."

Christian led Basil through a series of rooms (including a library full of books, which looked like the only "lived-in" room in the house) until they came to a very small, green-carpeted room with a TV, a chair, and a couch in it, darkened by closed blinds. A shriveled little woman sat in the chair, an afghan draped over her legs as she watched recorded soap opera reruns. Her mouth drooped open slightly and her eyes were glazed as the television light reflected on them. She barely moved a muscle as Basil and Christian came into the room.

"Hi, Gram," she said. The woman, who probably hadn't budged in at least a few hours, didn't even look up. She kept facing the television as her mouth turned into a half-smile.

"Hi, honey. Who do you have with you today?" She turned her head to glance at Basil.

"We're going to see if our classmate Anthony is okay. He hasn't been to school in two weeks and we're really worried about him." But by then, Gram had stopped listening, as it seemed that her attention was back on the television set. Christian sighed.

"What was that, dear?"

"I said we're going to visit our classmate Anthony to check on him. He hasn't been to school in a while and we're worried about him."

"That's fine, dear," she said, her eyes glazed over once again as she reentered her television fantasy-land.

"Gram," Christian sighed again as they left the room. "She's not my real grandmother—she's my step-dad's mom. She's kind of nice, but I don't think she cares for me too much," Christian said as they walked out to her garage to get her yellow three-speed bike. "Oh, well."

"Why don't you just go to your dad's house for the weekend?" Basil asked, hoping it wasn't a rude question. He hated it when people asked about his own father.

"Normally I would—I usually go to his house about two or three weekends a month. They live in the subdivision next to Birch Lakes—Birch View," she said. "But this weekend, Dad and my step-mom said they were too busy to have me. Dad said they needed to relax before their big lectures they both have on Monday, so they were going to take my half-sister Fiona to the club for the day."

"Oh. Sounds like a big weekend," Basil said sarcastically. "So why don't they take you, too?"

"They *claim* that it's too hard to come and get me when the country club is in the opposite direction of my mom's house," she said. "My parents hate driving—they say it's horrible for the environment, so they try to drive as little as possible, and every mile counts, my dad always says, even though I only live eight-tenths of a mile from their house—I measured it on a map one day.

Really, though, I think they just don't want me to spoil their day with little Princess Fiona. But anyway, it'll ruin my day to talk about it, so let's not, okay?"

"Sure," Basil said. "That sounds pretty horrible. But at least you talk to your dad—I don't even think my dad knows I exist."

"Really? Like, you've never even met him?"

"Well, I mean, not that I remember. He knows I was born, but since my parents got divorced he has almost totally ignored me. I don't even know what he looks like. I know he's remarried, and actually I think he has two little kids, which means I have little half-siblings too. I bet they're creepy and spoiled, like your sister."

"Probably," Christian said.

They got on their bikes and Basil led the way, leaving the riches of the Birch Lakes subdivision behind them as they headed to the darker side of town in the Skids.

"Did you ever call Shamus to ask him if he wanted to come?" Christian asked as they rode their bikes.

"No," Basil said. "I thought about it, and I just didn't think he'd be a good person to bring. He doesn't like Anthony very much."

"Good point," Christian agreed. "Well, I asked Sarah and Abbie if they wanted to come this morning. You know, strength in numbers. But Abbie said she has too much homework. Sarah really wanted to come, but she has some kind of all-day thing at her church. She told us she would pray for us," she added. "Figures."

Basil wasn't in a very talkative mood—he was, as usual, very distracted by his concerns for Anthony. He tried to prepare himself for the worst as the knot in his stomach twisted more and more painfully with anxiety over what they might find at Anthony's shack.

"Maybe we should check out Anthony's secret hiding spot first?" Basil said as they neared the street that led to his house.

"His secret hiding spot?" Christian said. "You mean he has another place he goes to?"

"Yeah, it's kind of near his house. You know, I was thinking maybe he went there or something, and that's why we haven't seen him. Maybe he's hiding out there to get away from his dad."

"Whatever you think," Christian said.

They stopped at the edge of the forest and found a spot to hide their bikes. They covered their bikes with some branches and started trekking through the deep forest. Basil only hoped he could remember how to find the farmhouse.

It took them some time, but finally they spotted the clearing through the trees, along with the dilapidated farmhouse that Anthony loved to spend time in. Basil tore through the remainder of the trees as Christian lectured him about being careful not to crush the "flora" while she tried to keep up. When they reached the clearing, they both broke into a run. The brilliant greens of the pasture were lit up against an impossibly blue sky. It was quite a sight to take in. But to Basil and Christian, only one thing was visible—the farmhouse that might have their helpless friend inside.

Basil stopped in his tracks just before the doorway of the house, worried about what he might find. While he hoped he would find his friend inside, maybe flipping through a book or feeding nuts to a squirrel in his lap—he knew that he could also find something upsetting, or nothing at all.

"Careful," Basil urged Christian. "We don't really know what we'll find in here."

"Good thinking," Christian agreed. They tiptoed forward, looking around them with every move. The house looked untouched since Basil had last seen it—the loose floorboard under which Anthony hid his things was in place. A bird hopped across the floor, and, noticing Basil and Christian, quickly flew out of a hole in the wall. The floorboards creaked beneath their footsteps. It was so quiet they were afraid to breathe. Basil went to Anthony's loose floorboard, with the hole just big enough for a small finger to slip through to pull it up. He pried it open. A mouse scurried away under the floorboard. Dust flew up into the air, catching in the sunlight streaming into the house through the windows.

"Oh, no," Basil said as he looked into the empty opening in the floor.

"What is it? What's wrong?" Christian said.

"Anthony's things are gone!" Basil said, feeling sick to his stomach. He turned to Christian.

"So what? What does that mean?" she said.

"I don't know. It might mean that he ran away. Or maybe someone stole his stuff, or maybe he took it back to his house," he said. "We need to go to his place. Maybe he's there."

Without wasting any time, they left the house and ran back through the forest to the road. Christian led the way this time—she had a remarkable memory, which was helpful when finding her way around a forest.

The trick to going to Anthony's house was finding a way to approach it unseen. There was a good chance that Anthony's father could be home, and of course an encounter with him could be dangerous.

"Let's sneak through the woods to the back of the house," Christian said. "Then we can watch for a while and see if we can spot anything through the windows."

They found a tree that had fallen in the woods just behind the house and sat on it. Christian pulled a small pair of binoculars from her army bag and took a look.

"What do you see?" Basil asked, hoping to use them himself.

"Nothing yet. It's hard to see much, because it's so dark in there. Wait, wait," she started whispering excitedly, "I see some movement. In that window, where the sun is shining—I see someone in there, sitting on a couch or something."

"Does it look like Anthony?"

"I can't tell. We'll have to go closer to see." Christian put the binoculars away, threw her bag over her shoulder and started moving toward the house.

"What are you *doing*?!" Basil whispered forcefully. "Do you want to get killed?"

"Come on, Basil, what are you afraid of? If this man is so bad, then Anthony's life is at stake, and we need to help him. Let's go."

Basil followed reluctantly and then crept up to the house, hiding behind an overgrown weed beside the window. Basil was petrified. Christian peered in the bottom corner of the window. Then she crouched down quickly. "Get down!" she whispered. "I think it's his dad!"

Basil's stomach turned to jelly. He felt faint. But Christian only stood up again and peeked in, reporting to Basil what she saw. "I see him—he's sitting down on a chair."

"What's he doing? Can he see you?" Basil asked.

"No, he can't. His face is in his hands. Actually—" She paused. "It looks like he's crying."

"Oh no. That can't be good," Basil said. "Do you see Anthony?"

"No," Christian said.

All the while, police sirens had been sounding off in the distance, sounding louder and louder by the second. It took a while before Basil and Christian realized that the sirens were headed right to Anthony's house.

Basil looked behind him and saw a flicker of red and blue through the trees—police cars were approaching. And not just one or two—about a half-dozen police cars came roaring up on the long gravel drive leading to the house. Basil and Christian froze.

"What should we do?"

"Get down! Quick!"

"I'm gonna run," Christian said.

They heard a slam of several car doors, feet crunching on the gravel, a fist pounding on the flimsy front door of the house, shouting.

"Open up, police!"

"I'm out of here!" Christian said as she began running. Basil had no choice—he started running after Christian, heading straight for the forest.

"Wait, kids! Come back!" A police officer waiting on the

driveway spotted Christian and Basil and began chasing them. He caught up to them quickly, grabbing Christian's arm. Christian struggled to get away, but when Basil saw that the policeman had grabbed her, he turned and came up to them.

❧ **Chapter 24**

"Relax, you two!" said the burly policeman, huffing to catch his breath from running after Basil and Christian. "I'm not going to hurt you. I just want to know what you saw in there." His tight grip on Christian's arm loosened. "Why don't you kids come back to my car and we can talk."

Neither Basil nor Christian wanted to get into any trouble. So they quietly went with him, their hearts racing as they walked back to his squad car. As they reached the car, they saw two large police officers walking out a drunken-looking, red-faced man, the few scraggly, greasy hairs on his head hanging loosely in his face, which was slumped down to his chest as he shuffled along, practically hanging on the two police officers' arms. They pushed his half-conscious body into the back seat of a squad car. He didn't resist.

"Why don't you guys get into the car, and we'll talk," the officer said.

"Are you going to take us to the station?" Christian asked.

"No, no," he said, smiling. "You're not in trouble, kids. I'm going to take you home. It's getting late and I don't want you two going home in the dark. How did you get here?"

"We rode our bikes," Basil said. "We left them in the trees off the road a ways."

"I have a lot of space in my trunk," said the officer. "How about I put the bikes in there and take them home for you?"

"What time is it?" Basil asked. He forgot that he was wearing a watch. He looked to see what time it was—5:30 P.M.

"Five-thirty! Yes, please drive us, officer. My mom gets home from work at five and she has this big thing about me being home when she gets home from work. She's going to kill me!"

"Yeah, I guess I should get home soon, too," Christian said.

"Well, hop in the car and I'll take you home. Just tell me where your bikes are and we'll go from there."

They got into the backseat of the car.

"So," Officer Mark asked them after they picked up the bikes, "what brought you kids to this jerk's house?"

"We know his son, Anthony, from school," Christian said. "We were worried about him because he hasn't been in school for a while, so we were going to check on him."

Officer Mark didn't say anything. He just kind of coughed and was silent.

"Hey, so Officer, can you tell us what happened?" Basil asked. "Do *you* know where Anthony is?"

"Sorry kids, I can't tell you that," he said. Basil and Christian were disappointed. "But I'm sure that soon enough you'll find out all about this guy in the newspapers."

Christian's eyes widened. They were afraid to ask any more questions.

"Do you think he killed Anthony?" Christian whispered to Basil while Officer Mark talked into his radio. Basil was speechless. His throat was dry, and he squeaked out an "I don't know." That was all he could say. His brain was swimming in a million anxieties.

"BASIL THEOPHILUS GOLD, you get in this house right now and start talking!" Basil's mom was furious. "Thank you, Officer," she said, trying to sound nice, before slamming the door shut and dragging Basil to a couch. "Here I am, ready to call the police to put out a search for my son, who is an hour late out doing who-knows-what, who-knows-where, when you come driving up *in a police car*! You *better* have a good reason for being so late!"

"Mom, gosh, just calm down, I wasn't out that late. It's only six o'clock!"

"Don't you tell me what's late and what isn't. I'm the mother in this family. You need to be home when I tell you to be home. I have told you a million times to stay at home when I'm at work on Saturdays unless I know where you are going to be."

"I know, Mom, but—" Basil blurted out.

"But nothing. What were you doing all day? I called here about ten times to talk to you and you weren't here."

"I went out," Basil said, not sure how to explain.

"Well, that's abundantly clear," Basil's mom said sarcastically. "So where did you go?"

"There's this kid from school named Anthony, Mom, and my friend Christian and I thought he might be in trouble, so we went to his house to see if he was okay."

"That's your excuse?" she said. "Look, I've had a really long day at work. You know very well that April is tax season, and I don't have time for this kind of garbage from you. I'm really strung out, okay? I don't think I can handle this much more." She didn't seem so angry anymore, just drained.

"But Mom, I was trying to help a friend! Doesn't that—"

"Basil, I don't care if you were trying to help the *president*—you could have gotten lost, kidnapped, or into some other kind of trouble. And I'll tell you another thing—I am getting *real* tired of you going all over creation doing whatever you please. And that *includes* your so-called research for your stories. If you can't write a good article without disobeying your mother, then you shouldn't be a journalist. You were supposed to stay home today and do algebra homework, not ride around stalking troubled kids from school! I'm getting sick of this hero-journalist thing—you are a kid, Basil, not a grown-up! While I'm around, you better not disobey me anymore. From now on I want to know where you are every *second*—and if you don't like that, *tough*. Take this as your last warning, Basil. And I am dead serious about this—no more doing whatever you please as if you didn't have a mother, or I will ground you for the rest of the school year."

"But—"

"*And,*" she went on, "I will make you quit the newspaper."

Basil was stunned. Never before had she made a threat like this—and knowing his mom, if she was in a bad enough mood the next time he made her mad, she would certainly follow through with her threat. His mom was moody like that—if she was in a good mood, it took a lot to upset her; but when she was in one of her down modes, she was impossible to be around.

Basil's vision was blurred by tears. He bit his tongue and clenched his fists to keep from talking back, spat out a "fine!" and ran up to his room. Mom always had to have the last word when she was in this kind of mood. So he half expected to hear her say something as he headed up the stairs. But she was quiet.

Basil lay on his bed all night, his mind replaying the horrors of the day. All the while, he couldn't help wondering if his friend Anthony was okay.

Chapter 25

MONDAY AT SCHOOL, Abbie told the other *News* kids the *Mittleton Sentinel* had reported that Anthony's dad was arrested after confessing to the murder of his wife.

"Here guys, check this out," Abbie said, laying a newspaper clipping on the lunch table.

"It says that Anthony ran away from home and mailed in his eyewitness account of his mother's murder—and get this! His dad did it! It also says Anthony sent a letter to his father telling him he'd turned him in," said Christian, who had grabbed the article and skimmed it, reporting to everyone what it said. "The police came and got his dad and took him to jail, where he 'awaits trial.' His father could go to prison for life! Wow."

"See," Abbie said to Shamus, "I told you his father killed his mother!"

"Let me see that!" Shamus said, grabbing the article from Christian's hands.

"Basil, do you realize what this means?" Christian said. "It means that when we snuck up on Anthony's house and saw his dad crying like that, he must have just read that letter. It's like he was just waiting for the police to come and get him."

"Man," Shamus said, "that's messed up. I wish I could have gone with you. You should have told me you were going! Oh, I know. You probably didn't want me to interrupt your 'date.'"

"Shut up, Shamus! It wasn't a date," Christian said. "And anyway, we didn't want to invite you. You hate Anthony."

"Yeah, but I still would have wanted to see the haunted house he lives in. What was it like?"

Basil was speechless. He was sickened about Anthony's dad

admitting to killing his mom, mad at Shamus for embarrassing him and being so cruel—he was beginning to see that Shamus and Farley were related, after all.

"It was a house, Shamus," Basil said, trying not to show his anger. "A small old house."

Things were getting tense. Sarah tried to change the subject.

"So, what are you going to write about for your next article?" she asked Basil.

Uh-oh. Basil had totally forgotten about his next story, due in two weeks. "I can't really say," he said.

"Oh, that's cool, if it's a secret and all," Shamus said, annoyed. "I guess our 'star reporter' can get away with keeping his stories a secret until he breaks them."

"Whatever," Basil said. Seconds later, the bell rang, and everyone scurried off to class.

ONE OF THE NICEST THINGS FOR BASIL about being at St. Norbert's was that the students, because of their admission into one of the highest-ranked private schools in the country, were allowed access to the local private college's extensive library stacks. To use the stacks, they had to submit a written request and receive special permission from the strict librarian, Ms. Weaver, who only allowed serious students to enter. The stacks contained some very old, priceless books, and in general this library was a sacred place for researchers of all stripes. One of Basil's goals as a young journalist was to master use of the libraries in town, and the stacks provided a challenging learning experience. Basil thought the college library would be a good place to come up with a story idea that would top all his previous stories. He was also tired of asking Father Maximos over and over for ideas.

Monday after school, Basil made a request to visit the stacks; on Tuesday, the librarian communicated her permission through Mr. Dixon. So on Tuesday after school, Basil biked to the nearby ivy-covered campus, his bike wheels wobbling on the old brick roads until he reached the massive library building. His mom was at work, so he didn't bother to ask her permission.

"Just be careful with these books—some of them are very, very old." Ms. Weaver grabbed his wrist tightly before he turned to enter. "Let me repeat—very, very old. And very precious." Her eyes blazed with passion over her books.

"I'll be careful," he said, tugging his wrist out of her grip and walking slowly through the entryway into the stacks. Inside were more books than a person could imagine, in a maze-like and suffocatingly cramped sort of place. He was searching for books on mysteries and miracles, hoping to find something that would lead him to a modern miracle he could write about. Finally he found a wide section of books on ancient and new mysteries and unexplained phenomena.

The Shroud of Turin. Appearances of the Virgin Mary. UFOs, occurrences of stigmata, weeping icons, the seven ancient mysteries of the world, the Bible code, Arthurian folklore and the Holy Grail, witchcraft, paganism, the occult, the Book of Revelation and the Apocalypse—there were so many books and topics to choose from, so many enticing mysteries to explore. Basil sat for about two hours flipping through a pile of books. As he browsed, he felt eerily alone in the quiet, old-book smelliness of the stacks. The longer he sat there reading about such frightful things, the more paranoid he grew. He began looking over his shoulder every few seconds, catching a shadow out of the corner of his view and thinking someone was watching him.

He made a list of possible topics, all of which he was less than enthusiastic about. He considered writing an article about something like the Shroud of Turin (the ancient cloth imprinted with an inexplicable image of Jesus' face), or maybe the vision of the Virgin Mary at Fatima, a haunting tale of an appearance of Jesus' mother. He was fascinated by such things. But still, as a journalist he knew that his story would have to have some kind of newsworthiness; it needed some kind of local connection. If he did write a story about an international miracle or mystery, he would have to interview some kind of expert. He doubted that he would be able to call one of the European scholars who studied the Shroud or the Fatima visions with his mother's permission—surely such a call would cost a fortune, not to mention the language problem. He wanted to find a local story; he was stumped.

Basil thanked the librarian for letting him browse the stacks. He checked out a few books on the Shroud of Turin and left.

BASIL DIDN'T REALLY FEEL RIGHT doing a story on the Shroud; not that it wasn't an interesting story—it's just that he had hoped to do articles on current miracles, rather than on unsolved mysteries. Still, he was desperate for a story, and the deadline was fast approaching.

The night before his article was due, he flipped through the books he had borrowed from the stacks, sat down and typed out an article. He wasn't proud of his work, but at least he would have something to turn in while he fretted about other things—his algebra grades were getting worse, rather than better; Shamus was keeping his distance and always seemed irritated with him; and of course he couldn't help but wonder what had happened to Anthony.

Basil turned in his article, hoping not to draw too much attention to himself, as he was a little embarrassed about his procrastination and hoped no one would notice that it wasn't his best article.

That weekend was Easter. Basil wanted to go to Holy Resurrection for the service; Father Maximos told him that the Easter service at their church was different—very late at night and very exciting. In fact, often even the date of Easter was different in the Orthodox Church, but this year the Western date and the Orthodox date happened to coincide. Father Maximos said the service would start with a dark church at midnight on Easter eve and end with a huge feast at two in the morning, in celebration of Jesus' resurrection from the dead.

But of course, Basil's mom refused to take him to a church service that late at night; instead, they ended up going to the generic church they always went to on Christmas and Easter. They arrived late, left early, and then went out to breakfast at the Pancake House, the restaurant they always went to on special occasions. But this year, Basil's favorite chocolate chip pancakes, cooked up specially for him by Guy, the Pancake House's chef and owner, didn't taste nearly as good as usual with all that he had on his mind.

May

❁ Chapter 26

BASIL WASN'T SURPRISED WHEN MR. DIXON kept him after the newspaper meeting the last week of April, on the day that the April edition, with Basil's Shroud of Turin article, was released to the students.

"Basil, I want to talk to you for a second," he said as the other staffers were clearing out to go home. "Is everything all right? I hesitated to bring this up, but I was a little disappointed with your last article."

Basil looked away from Mr. Dixon's prodding eyes. Mr. Dixon went on, "The readers liked it, but to be honest I thought it read like a book report. What's going on? Are you losing your enthusiasm?"

"I don't know . . . I really just procrastinated, Mr. Dixon," Basil said. "I didn't have a good story idea for this one."

"Why didn't you ask me for help?" Mr. Dixon said. "You should have asked weeks before the deadline, instead of not asking and throwing something together at the last minute. That's not how good journalists work, Basil."

"Yeah, I know I should have asked, Mr. Dixon. But I was really distracted."

"Distracted with what? Is your home life okay?"

"Well, sort of. I'm kind of worried about what's going on with Anthony."

"Ah—Anthony." Mr. Dixon paused. "Why don't we sit down for a minute and talk about this." They each took a seat at two of the empty desks in the room.

"There, that's better. You know, I'm worried about Anthony, too. There are rumors, of course—not just flying from student to

129

student—we teachers have heard rumors, too. Legally, I'm not sure if there is much we can do. And since no one really knows how to find out where he is . . . well, let's just say that hopefully, the authorities know what's going on."

"Mr. Dixon," Basil said, taking a deep breath, "do you think Anthony's been hurt? Do you think he's—do you think he's dead?"

"I'm sure the news hounds at the *Mittleton Sentinel* would have broken that story if it were true. No, I don't think he's hurt. I'm guessing he's in the care of family, but of course the police are being very 'hush hush' about everything."

"Yeah, I know," Basil said.

"Well listen, Basil. Don't worry about Anthony. I'm sure the truth will come out soon enough. Just keep praying for him, and in the meantime, don't start slipping on your responsibilities as a student, and as our star reporter." He gave Basil a friendly wink and nudge. "We only have one issue left, and I need you to help us pull this off. You are an impressive reporter—you've done things that even much older kids aren't capable of. I have a lot of faith in your abilities, and I want you to do your best."

"Yeah, but that's the other thing, Mr. Dixon. My mom has been on my back lately about my math grades, and she said if I don't start doing better and stop getting into trouble she'll make me quit the paper."

"Hmmm . . . well, that wouldn't be good. Why are you getting into trouble?"

"Well, I've been late a few times coming home, and I went out when I wasn't supposed to—mostly working on articles and that kind of stuff."

"Basil, you shouldn't have to get in trouble to write a good story. I'll tell you what—if you need help coming up with ways to talk to sources and gather information, I'm sure I can help you. If it's a matter of money, we have enough in our budget to pay for a few long-distance calls, if necessary."

Basil brightened up a bit. "Okay!"

"Oh, and Basil, if your mom is angry at you right now, maybe

I could talk with her—I'm sure I could make a pretty good case for why you should be allowed to stay on our staff. And if she needs someone to crack down on you about your math grades, well, I can do that, too." He smiled.

"Well, hopefully it won't come to that—I hear you can be pretty tough when you want to be, Mr. Dixon."

"Ha! If only that were true! Everyone knows I'm a softie. But oh well." He looked at his watch. "You should go before you get in trouble again. When you get home, tell your mom I'm going to give her a call tonight or tomorrow night to talk about this."

"Thanks!" Basil said. For a moment, he almost forgot about his worries.

⁘ Chapter 27

MR. DIXON SPOKE WITH BASIL'S MOM and sang Basil's praises; as a result (and probably also because spring was in the air, taxes were filed, and she was in a great mood) Basil's mom softened toward his involvement with the paper.

Of course, that didn't help Basil come up with a story idea for the May issue. There are only so many miracles one can write about in a year's time, he thought, so how would he find another? He didn't want to have to keep asking Father Maximos—he feared he was becoming a pest. Then again, he didn't want to wait until the last minute, as he had with his last article, to come up with an idea.

But then, as usual, Father Maximos rescued him.

"How are your articles coming along, Basil?" Father Maximos asked him as they nibbled on bagels after church in early May.

"They're great—people have really been talking about them, and I've gotten a lot of compliments," he said.

"Good, good," said Father Maximos.

"But," Basil said, "it's just that I can't think of anything else to write about."

"You can't think of anything else?" asked Father Maximos, seeming surprised. "Why, I can think of a thousand stories, if not ten thousand. You hear of many miraculous things as an old priest."

"Yeah, but I kind of wanted to write about something really recent, or at least somewhat local," Basil said.

"Oh, well, that certainly narrows it down. Let's see. Do you have to write about a certain kind of experience, or could you broaden your approach a little bit?"

"What do you mean?"

"I'm thinking of a local man who had a life-changing experience which would be quite interesting to write about, although nothing outwardly miraculous happened. I wouldn't say his conversion wasn't a miracle, though—it certainly was."

"What's the story?" Basil asked, feeling his frustration start to fade.

"It's a very moving story, really—a few years ago, a wealthy community leader disappeared one day after giving his multimillion-dollar fortune to local charities. But he really only disappeared in the eyes of the world—in reality, he had left the world behind to become a monk at our local monastery. This man, who became Father Isaac, was in his old life an amazing Renaissance man. He had degrees in both medicine and law. He had written several books of poetry and had a successful career in the evenings as a violin player. He made his living as a lawyer, but got rich trading stocks, often dining with presidents of large corporations. Then, after a family tragedy drove him to reevaluate life, the man came to the church looking broken, asking for help. He saw the weeping icon and then approached me in tears, confessing every sin he had ever committed. At the end of the confession, he said nothing more, except that he was going to move to a newly built monastery in the wilderness outside of town, and that he planned to become a monk, living in solitude and prayer. He made arrangements immediately to sell all his possessions and enter the monastery that very same week. He has been there ever since."

"So is he at the monastery that Mr. Ammar built?"

"Yes, that is it—Mr. Ammar told you about it, then?"

"Yeah—he told me his whole story."

"Wonderful—he is a remarkable man, too," Father Maximos said. "But I think you will be no less impressed by Father Isaac's story. Let me stress that while his story may not seem to you like a miracle of a supernatural nature, I urge you to think about this story as a miracle of a different kind. Think about how hard it would be to give away millions of dollars to the poor, and you will soon realize that this really *is* a miracle from God. The whole town, from the media to his colleagues and friends, were stunned when he sold everything and gave the money away. One story I remember reading told of how the Mayor himself rushed to this man's estate the morning he found out, hoping to sway him to reconsider. But by then, Father Isaac was gone, of course, off to the monastery. And once he was there, Abbot Isidore was very firm about not letting anyone see him, at Father Isaac's own request. Reporters even stayed outside the monastery grounds for weeks, before finally giving up and going home—they never got one picture of him, because from what Abbot Isidore told me, Father Isaac stayed inside his cell for months before ever leaving. Now, it's as if the world has completely forgotten the man—no one ever speaks of him. Interesting, huh?"

"Yeah, wow," remarked Basil. "So what made him do it?"

"That would be a question to ask him," Father said.

"Ask him? You mean he would let me talk to him when he wouldn't even let the real reporters interview him?"

"I think you'd be surprised—Father Isaac has been at the monastery for a while now, and I already spoke with him, thinking this might be a good article for you. He said he would let you do it."

"Wow," Basil said. "That would be awesome!"

"Do you know how to find the monastery?"

"Actually, I think I saw it—I think it's on the other side of the forest by my house," he said.

"Well, just in case you don't know how to get there, let me draw you a map and give you the monastery's phone number. You may need to have your mother drive you there—it might be hard to get to because the forest can be dense, and it completely surrounds the monastery. Don't try to go there on your bike," he said, knowing Basil took his bike everywhere and was almost always unaccompanied by his mom.

"Okay, Father Maximos," Basil said, getting up to leave.

⚘ Chapter 28

"BACK AGAIN?" THE LIBRARIAN ASKED as Basil came up to the information desk at the university library the next Tuesday. Basil had to make up for the weakness of his last article. He decided before he rushed off to the monastery to meet Father Isaac, he would see if he could find some old newspaper articles on his disappearance.

But where would he start?

He approached the librarian, thinking maybe she'd know how he could find newspaper clippings.

"Hi, Ms. Weaver," he started. "I need to do research for another article for my school paper."

"How might I help?" she asked.

"Well, I'm looking for information about a man who became a monk. I heard it was big news a few years ago."

"Hmmm . . . that sounds familiar," she said. "Do you know his name? If you knew, we could look it up in our database."

Basil drew a blank. He knew the man's name as a monk was Father Isaac, but that surely wasn't his name when he was in the "world" as a lawyer. "I'm—I'm not sure, actually," he said.

"Let me think," said Ms. Weaver, playing with the chain on her glasses. "Why don't you tell me more about the story and maybe I'll remember it. I've been around this town for quite a while."

"Okay, let's see," Basil said. "I remember that the guy was a big businessman, very rich, and one day some kind of family tragedy made him go crazy, so he sold all his things . . ."

"And moved to a monastery. Yes, okay, I do know whom you are talking about. That is indeed a famous story. His name was Anthony Porfirio." Her fingers flew quickly over the keys of her computer as she started searching the database for articles about him.

"Yes, yes," she said, looking up and down the computer screen as she mumbled to herself. "Hmmm . . . Yes, here we go. This is it. There are several articles here in our database. Would you like me to print some out for you?"

"Yeah, thanks!" Basil said. Ms. Weaver printed out a few articles and handed them to Basil, who sat down at a nearby table and started to read.

MITTLETON Anthony Porfirio of Porfirio, O'Malley and Smith law firm disappeared Saturday after selling all his possessions and distributing the money between several prominent charities in the Mittleton area.

Porfirio, 45, was a prominent local figure with an estimated net worth of $1.5 billion; he gave most of his estate to a selection of local charitable organizations, including churches and organizations such as the Kid's Club and Emergency Nursery, a local organization that provides temporary housing for children in need.

After his sister Maria Camarata died tragically of a head injury, Porfirio suffered a nervous breakdown.

"We're not exactly sure what happened," said Mayor Quigley, a former business partner and friend of Porfirio. But we re all devastated by his decision to leave public life, and we re just trying to understand why he needed to take such drastic measures to recover from the tragedy of his sister's death. We hope he comes home soon.

Quigley and other friends report that Porfirio, after giving away his fortunes, retreated to the local Monastery of Saint Vasily, where he leads a life of solitude and prayer.

Neither Porfirio nor Saint Vasily Monastery responded to the Mittleton Sentinel's requests for interviews.

The article was dated two years ago; Basil couldn't figure out why the story struck him as being so familiar. Maybe he had seen stories about it on the evening news. He read the article a second time, then a third. The other articles were similar—apparently very little was known about what happened, and while different articles featured different friends and colleagues commenting on Mr. Porfirio's disappearance, the information was all the same.

Suddenly, Basil's eye lit on the name of Mr. Porfirio's sister, Maria Camarata. His stomach twisted into a knot over that name. His heart started racing, and he felt so excited he almost jumped out of his skin.

Anthony's last name was Camarata—Maria must be his mother! Information started flooding into Basil's mind. Anthony had said his mom's name was Maria—the kids at school said she died from a head injury after she fell down the stairs. That meant that Father Isaac must be Anthony's uncle.

This meant only one thing to Basil, and it had nothing to do with a profile on Father Isaac. It meant that if anyone knew where Anthony had disappeared to, it would surely be Father Isaac.

With that, he crammed the articles into his backpack and practically ran out the door.

"Oh, please," Ms. Weaver called after him, shaking her head and tsk'ing, "no running in the library, Basil!"

⁙ Chapter 29

BASIL TRIED TO PAY ATTENTION in classes that week. He couldn't afford another bad algebra grade on a quiz. But it was hard to focus in his classes while his mind kept devising schemes for getting to the monastery. He hadn't told anyone all week at school about what he'd learned about Anthony's uncle. But finally, he couldn't keep it in anymore. On Friday afternoon in Mrs. Santi's class, Basil wrote down on a piece of paper what he'd found out about Anthony's uncle, and how he planned to find the monastery the next day. He folded up the piece of paper and passed it to Christian. He wasn't necessarily asking her to go with him (that could be considered a "date," and he'd already made that mistake once), but he figured if she wanted to go with him, maybe she would call.

Christian took the note just as Mrs. Santi turned around from a timeline she was drawing on the blackboard. She stared at Christian and Basil. Christian quickly crammed the note inside her desk. Mrs. Santi raised an eyebrow in suspicion and then returned to her lecture. When the bell rang, Christian took the note out and started reading it.

"Bye, Christian," Basil said, heading out the door to go home.

"Wait, Basil!" he heard Christian shout as he left.

THE NEXT DAY, SATURDAY, his mom was working—she wouldn't be home until five o'clock. It was a warm and sunny spring day— that afternoon would be the perfect time for an attempt at a hike over to the Saint Vasily Monastery on the other side of the forest.

Basil picked up the phone to call Christian, but there was no answer at her place. So he dumped his books out of his backpack and instead packed away a pen and notebook, a bottle of water, binoculars, and a few other odds and ends that might come in handy on a hike.

Just then, the phone rang. Basil hesitated to answer it—but what if it was Christian? He picked it up.

"Hello?"

"Hi, it's Mom," she said, sounding like she was in a good mood.

"Hi, Mom," Basil said, fretting as if he'd been caught in the act, and then feeling guilty that he was about to lie to his mom about his afternoon plans.

"Hey, I only have a second, but can you do me a favor and take some chicken out of the freezer to thaw so I can make it for dinner? I was thinking of making chicken teriyaki when I get home."

"Sure," Basil said.

"Oh, and make sure you keep working on your algebra. We don't want the *St. Norbert News* star reporter to get bad math grades, or else," she said, sounding light-hearted.

Eek. How to get around this one? "Sure mom, I'll do the algebra."

"Oh, there's my boss, I gotta go," Mom said. "I'll be home around five-fifteen. Love you!"

BASIL PAUSED BEFORE LEAVING THE HOUSE, momentarily thinking he'd be better off tossing his plans and spending the afternoon with his algebra books—after all, he'd get his studying done and would eliminate the risk of disobeying his mom. Christian had never called, and he wasn't sure he wanted to go alone. But then he looked out the window into the dense forest, and an adventure beckoned. He threw his backpack over his shoulder, slid the back door open, and trekked through his backyard to the edge of the forest.

At first, it was easy. He had been hiking in the forest before, so he sort of knew his way around. But after about thirty minutes, he had wandered farther than he ever had before, and at that point he really wished Christian, the nature enthusiast and hiker extraordinaire, were with him as a guide. He tried to follow the sun, but he could barely find it in the sky through the trees. He had a compass, so he pulled it out and tried to head east, but he wasn't exactly sure that the monastery was due east. Unsure, he kept going deeper, hoping his gut would lead him in the right direction.

As he approached a small clearing in the trees with a stream, he sat down to rest in the tall grass, pulling another snack out of his backpack. He glanced at his watch as he munched and nearly choked on his food—it was four o'clock! That meant he only had an hour and fifteen minutes to find the monastery (and Father Isaac) and get home before his mom got home from work and found him missing. Just as he picked up his backpack, he heard some branches snap behind him. He jumped up and whirled around.

"Boo!" Christian said, laughing. "Man, I scared you, didn't I!"

"What are you doing here?" Basil said. "I didn't think you were coming."

"Well, I thought I would surprise you."

"How did you find me?"

"Easy," she said. "You left a trail of candy wrappers behind you. Shame on you for littering!"

Basil laughed. "Wow, you're good. I can't even figure out where I am."

"We better hurry. It's getting late. I think we're pretty close, though. I looked up the monastery on the map, and it should be a few hundred more feet that way." She pointed east.

"Let's go, then!" he said.

They started walking east, stumbling over fallen branches, toward Saint Vasily's. As they walked, the winds picked up, getting colder. The sky was darkening, and Basil wasn't sure if it was from the setting of the sun or a storm blowing in. Then they felt rain-drops.

"Great, just what we need," Christian said. "Rain."

Moments later, they saw a clearing through the trees, and in the distance what looked like a large pond. On the other side of the pond was a gray stone building.

Terrified about how quickly time was slipping away, and yet spurred on by how close they were, they broke into a run, tearing through the forest until they nearly collapsed when they reached the forest's edge. Basil stopped for a second, thinking he might have asthma because of how hard he was panting trying to catch his breath. Between gasps, he looked up and saw a man across the pond, throwing breadcrumbs to geese.

The man looked like a priest or a monk—he was wearing a long black robe and a large cross around his neck. He had a medium-length beard and blondish-gray hair and looked about 45 or 50 years old. Basil and Christian weren't sure if they should approach the monk or not; they took a few steps toward him and then decided they might as well go up to him and ask for help. The raindrops were beginning to get heavier, so they would need shelter from the rain anyway, and maybe rides home.

The man looked up and noticed them. He didn't flinch at all at the sight of two kids coming out of the forest.

"Hello," he said, his voice softer than fleece, his eyes large and peaceful.

"Hi," said Basil, still somewhat out of breath. "My name is Basil, and I'm—"

"Yes, I know who you are," said the monk. "It's starting to rain. Why don't we go sit inside?"

"Are you Father Isaac?"

"Yes," he said serenely.

They walked in silence up a tall, green hill toward an old stone building that looked like a church. On the domed rooftop was a shining cross—no doubt the one Basil had seen from his window at home. They entered the building just as the rain started to pour down. Basil's heart sank as he wondered how on earth he would get home without his mom knowing he had

been gone all afternoon on an adventure instead of studying math.

Father Isaac led him to a room with a few couches by a fireplace—he called it the common area, and it was next to a dining room that held a long wooden table. Father Isaac started a fire in the fireplace.

Basil and Christian sat down next to each other on a couch; Basil nervously fiddled with his backpack, looking around him at his surroundings. Father Isaac sat down on the opposite couch, not saying a word. Another monk walked in from another room carrying a tray with teacups and a kettle. Without asking, he set two cups on the end table next to Basil and Christian and poured them some sweet tea. Father Isaac didn't say anything. He just stared at Basil. After a moment, he said quietly, "So you're here to learn about my story—where do you want to begin?"

Basil opened his mouth to speak, but before he could squeak out a word a small person with straw-colored hair came out of a doorway and sat quietly on the couch next to Father Isaac.

Basil had to blink to make sure his eyes were working. Could it be? Christian and Basil looked at each other in shock.

"Anthony?" Basil said. "What are you *doing* here? The whole school thinks you're in an orphanage somewhere! What happened?" Christian was wide-eyed and silent.

Anthony and Father Isaac looked calm. Father Isaac put his arm lovingly around Anthony's shoulders and gave him a pat.

"Why don't I explain, Basil," said Father Isaac. "Let me tell you my story, and then hopefully everything will fall into place."

Basil nodded, and took out his notebook to write things down.

"Oh, but please, no notes. I'd prefer that this not be written down. I don't mind if you want to write my story, but I think you will learn more if you just listen."

Basil reluctantly put his notebook away and dropped his hands awkwardly onto his lap. He glanced at his watch—four-forty-five. Maybe he could still make it home in time. He cleared his throat nervously and looked at Father Isaac.

"So I hear my friend and brother Father Maximos has told you a little bit about what happened," began Father Isaac. "Yes, I was once very rich, and very successful by the world's standards. I had many friends. I grew up this way. I was always popular, always rich and talented. My little sister Maria and I went to a private school. Our father was a successful restaurateur who owned a small group of fine restaurants in the area. As you may have heard, I went to medical school, but when I first became a doctor, I couldn't handle the death I constantly saw working in the emergency room, so I went to law school and became a lawyer. Then I started my own law firm.

"My sister also went to medical school, but dropped out when she met Hal Camarata, a boy who bussed tables at one of our restaurants. Hal was from a poor family, but Maria fell hopelessly in love with him. Our family disowned her when she ran off and married him. I, however, loved my sister too much not to give her husband a chance, so I befriended Hal. He was rough around the edges, but he had a good heart, I thought."

Christian, Basil, and Anthony sat and listened in front of the flickering firelight as Father Isaac told them his story. Basil forgot completely that it was quickly nearing five o'clock.

"But as Hal got older, something changed in him. At first he was a hot-blooded but fairly innocent young man, hard-working and charming. But then he started drinking nearly every day after work. And the more he drank, the angrier and more temperamental he became. My sister came to me crying on more than one occasion with bruises on her face and arms, saying Hal was hitting her. This began even before young Anthony was born, but of course, as much as I tried to get my sister to leave him and come to stay with me, she said she wanted to give him another chance, because she loved him. And when he was in a good mood, she said, he treated her like a princess. And of course, when the baby came, she had more reasons to stay—she didn't want to be on her own with a baby. She said her child needed his father, even with all his flaws. She was very forgiving."

Anthony looked down, biting his lip to avoid crying. Basil felt very bad for him.

"The drinking only got worse with time. Soon there was a time when Hal wouldn't come home for days, drinking and gambling

147

their money away. Maria of course had help from me, but this didn't prevent the abuse. And the more I gave her money, the more she got hit by Hal. He became insanely jealous of me. During some of his drunken rages, he blamed my sister's beatings on her proud, rich upbringing and her meddling brother. Around that time she started seeking solace and comfort in the church, and this further infuriated Hal, who hated that she depended on anything other than him. I tried to interfere, but Hal was a large man, very powerful, and he nearly strangled me a few times. But more frightening than this was the fact that if I interfered too much, he would beat her more. I felt trapped.

"When he killed Maria by pushing her down the stairs of their home, I lost my mind with guilt. It was then that I gave away everything I had and came here to become a monk, taking the spiritual name of Isaac. I refused to let anyone talk me out of it, and believe me, they tried. But I held fast, and eventually the cameras and the reporters went away, and my friends stopped calling the monastery. The world quickly forgot about me, which was a blessing. And it is here that I have spent the last three years making peace with God, and praying fervently for Hal, that he might change his ways."

"What about Anthony? What happened with him and his dad?"

"Anthony was taken away from his father when his mother died, but when Hal was acquitted of killing Maria for lack of evidence, Anthony was given back to his father. They went bankrupt from legal fees, so they lost the house and moved to the shack in the woods, where Anthony's dad spent less time working and even more time drinking. And with Maria gone, Hal had no one to control and push around other than Anthony, so he started laying into him, too. It was devastating for me, because once again I feared that Hal would try to kill Anthony if I stepped in. But before I could wait any longer, Hal beat Anthony almost to death, a month or so ago."

Basil glanced over at Anthony, who was staring at the wooden floor, a dark and lonely look on his face. "When Anthony regained

148

some of his strength," he continued, "he took what little he had and walked all the way to the monastery. He went to a gas station and asked where the monastery was, and then walked here through a spring rainstorm, so determined was he to get away from Hal.

"When he came to me, I knew it was time to make my final case against Hal. I knew God would provide us with an answer, a resolution to this tragedy. Anthony showed me his mother's journals, which detailed much of the abuse. In fact, in her very last journal entry, she wrote of how she was planning to leave Hal. Apparently, he discovered her journal while she was at church one morning, went to the church to get her, brought her home, and beat her to death. I never really knew any details about what happened—no one did, except Anthony, who was too young and scared to figure out how to tell us. After years of silence, I called a trusted friend, my old law partner, who was very surprised and overjoyed to hear from me, and together we came up with a case that held enough water to land Hal in jail.

"Believe me, it was not my goal to destroy the man. I have spent years praying that God will help me forgive him for what he did to my sister and nephew. But the man is quite sick and in need of healing. I will pray that when he spends time in prison, he will change. I received legal custody of Anthony. We are educating him here at the monastery, so he will no longer be going to St. Norbert's Academy. And he will finally be able to begin the healing process after years of abuse, neglect, and suffering. Glory be to God."

Anthony looked so happy and yet so sad at the same time. He was clean—his golden hair shimmered, his skin no longer had discolored patches from almost-healed bruises. He was wearing plain but clean clothes. He looked almost, well, *normal.*

"Wow—that's amazing. I'm really happy to hear that you're safe now, Anthony," Basil said.

"Yeah. But it's too bad you won't be on the *St. Norbert News* staff anymore. We'll miss your artwork. You'll have to mail us some of your drawings so we can still use them," Christian said.

"Thanks. Maybe I will," Anthony said.

"And you are all welcome to visit Anthony whenever you want," said Father Isaac.

"That would be cool," Basil said. "So, I hope this doesn't sound weird, but would you be okay with me writing a story on this for *St. Norbert News?*"

"I have given that some thought, and I have decided after much prayer that you may write on this, as long as you use your best judgment when telling this story," said Father Isaac. "You are the only journalist I've ever spoken to about this." Basil swelled with pride when Father Isaac called him a journalist. "I'll trust God will put the right words into your article."

"You will? Wow, thanks," said Basil.

"One more thing, though," Father Isaac went on. "Anthony has shown me all of your stories, and I love them—I think you are a very gifted young person. But try not to get carried away with miracles. Don't let your belief hinge on miracles, Basil. Let it hinge on faith. Blessed are those who don't see, and yet believe."

Basil nodded.

"I think the real miracle here is how you have been enlightened and how you've grown as a person because of this assignment you have been doing for the school paper," Father Isaac continued. "Don't you see, Basil? God gave you this assignment as a way of showing *you* the truth. Isn't it incredible how life works? To see all the coincidences, the sequence of events that causes everything to fall into place?" He paused, looking Basil straight in the eyes, and said with fire, "God is truly mysterious, truly awe-inspiring."

"Would you like some more tea?" The other monk came out of the kitchen and filled Basil and Christian's cups again with more sweet tea. It was then that Basil glanced out the window—the rain was still drumming on the windows, but now it was dark outside.

Basil had been so wrapped up in Father Isaac's story he had completely forgotten to watch the time. Now he glanced at his watch. It was almost five-thirty.

Basil started to panic. All he could think about was that his life would be over the moment he got home. He supposed there was a chance that if someone could drive him home, maybe his mom would be late and wouldn't catch him out.

"Oh my gosh, Father Isaac, I'm really late—is there any way you can drive us home?"

"Why don't you call home first and let your parents know that you'll be late," said Father Isaac, handing Basil a phone. "Then I will drive you."

"Thanks," he said, afraid to dial. He got up as the phone was ringing and paced nervously.

"Hello?" his mom answered. He could hear the worry in her voice.

"Hi, Mom," he said.

"Basil? Where *are* you?" She sounded mad. Very mad.

"I'm at a monastery near our house," he said. "One of the monks is going to drive me home."

"Get home *now!*" she screamed. "No, wait. I'm coming to get you. Don't move a muscle. I'll be there in five minutes."

Basil told her where to come to pick him up. Then she hung up on him without even saying goodbye.

When Basil's mom arrived minutes later, she barely stopped the car to pick him up. She didn't even speak a word in the car. When they got home, she threw her keys on the counter in the kitchen, went to the living room, sat down on a couch, and began sobbing. Basil tried to comfort her, but she pushed him away.

"Get out of my sight," she said. Basil wasn't sure if he should obey her, so he went into the kitchen, although he was too tired and stressed to eat.

A few minutes later she came into the kitchen and hugged him.

"I'm sorry I pushed you away," she said, crying. "You're all I've got, Basil. I just want you to be safe. And I'm so, so angry and hurt that you disobey me again and again."

"I'm sorry, Mom, I really didn't mean to, but—"

"Basil, there aren't any 'buts'," she said. "When I ask you to do

151

something, you do it. And if you want to do something special, something you don't think I'd want you to do, *ask me* first. I'm more angry that you didn't ask me."

"But you said you didn't like me going all over doing research for my articles," he said.

"Well, normally that's true. But maybe if you asked me first, I might say yes. You won't know unless you try, Basil. I think that's what hurts the most here—that my son won't talk to me about what he does or cares about."

Basil's mom was unusually soft and reasonable—perhaps because she was so tired of always yelling. But then came the clincher.

"You are grounded until I decide otherwise, and that includes doing any more research for the paper. I want you to go to school and come home, and that's it."

Basil was crushed. He felt his mother was persecuting him and couldn't understand why. He went to his room, slammed the door as hard as he could, and didn't come out for the rest of the night.

❀ Chapter 30

THE FOLLOWING WEEK, BASIL mostly sulked in his room, coming home right after school to work on algebra homework and read novels. He and his mom weren't on the best of terms, and he had one more article, for the last edition of the paper, due that week. The school year was almost over, but still, even a weekend of grounding for a kid is torture, much less three weeks.

Wednesday at school, Mr. Dixon held Basil after class, saying he'd noticed that something was "off" with Basil's mood. Basil told him the entire story.

"Basil, I'm sorry you got in trouble—but you really should have asked your mom's permission before you went off to the monastery. You need to start communicating better with her," Mr. Dixon said.

"Yeah, I guess," Basil said, feeling irritated that Mr. Dixon would side with his mom.

"Look, I think the solution is clear here. Use your time being grounded to write the best story you've ever written. To me, this is a no-brainer. You have all the research already, and you even have permission from Father Isaac to write a story that the professional journalists couldn't get. Even I'm a little jealous of you getting this story, Basil, and darn proud of you. So go home today and start writing. I have a feeling that once this all comes out, and your mom sees your motives were pure, it will be a new beginning for you and her. But you need to promise me that you will start communicating with her. I need you to stay on this staff, Basil. You're my—"

"Your star reporter, I know, Mr. Dixon," said Basil. "Okay, I'll go home and try to write something. It might take a while—I'm not sure how to get this all on paper."

"You have a little time left," Mr. Dixon said. "Our deadline is Thursday, but I'll give you until Monday to get me your article, since I know this will be a good one."

"Really? That would be awesome!"

"Yeah, go for it—I know you won't let me down."

"I hope not," said Basil.

Basil finally started understanding what writer's block was—he was paralyzed as he tried to write about Father Isaac and Anthony. Friday came and went, and then Saturday. His mother wasn't speaking to him much—she was still angry about the incident last weekend. By Saturday evening, Basil couldn't take the silence anymore. As their forks quietly clinked on their plates during a dinner of meatloaf, Basil broke the silence.

"Mom, I haven't been to church in a while now. So I was wondering, can I go tomorrow? I know I'm grounded, but this is church. It's not like I'm going to a party or anything."

Basil's mom was quiet for a moment, fiddling with the food on her plate.

"Okay," she said. "But I'm going with you."

Basil was relieved. He smiled, happy that the awful tension between them was finally breaking.

The service the next morning was long, as usual, but Basil's mom didn't seem bored. Rather, she seemed intrigued with all the sights and sounds and smells. She was moved by the weeping icon—it had stopped weeping a week earlier, but the tear stains were still there. During the fellowship hour, Basil introduced his mom to Father Maximos. She loved him.

As they sat at a table eating lemon cake, Father Maximos asked about Basil's visit to the monastery. Basil worried that it was a sore spot with his mom, but she said she was interested in knowing what he was doing there, now that she had cooled off a bit. So Basil told them both all about his visit.

"You know, Basil, you drive me crazy," she said later in the car. "I never knew what a great kid you really are. I've been so busy with work—it's my fault that I don't spend more time with you. From now on, I want to be more involved in your life."

"Really?"

"Yes," she said. "And don't worry—I'm not going to meddle or anything—but I want to read your articles and talk about what's going on with you. I love you, Basil, and I'm very proud of you." Tears were streaming down her cheeks.

"Thanks, Mom," Basil said. "And I'm sorry I've been such a pain for you. I want to do better, and I want to listen to you and help you more and stuff."

"That's okay, Basil. I understand—and I forgive you. And I hope you forgive me for the mistakes I've made, too."

"You don't make any mistakes, Mom," Basil said, smiling.

"You're sweet, but wrong," she said, laughing.

Resolving things with his mom was just what Basil needed to rejuvenate his desire to write his final column of the year for *St. Norbert News*. As soon as they got home, he went up to his room and started typing.

THE LAST THURSDAY IN MAY, near the end of the last full week of school, Basil sat at the lunch table watching students pass out copies of the last issue of *St. Norbert News*. The lunchroom seemed a little quieter as students sat glued to the pages of the award-winning paper that had gotten Basil so much attention as a new student that year. He nervously walked over to the table where Sarah and Christian sat passing out copies to students.

"Basil, omigosh. Your story—it's just amazing," Sarah said. Christian nodded in agreement.

"Yeah, I don't know what to say, Basil," Christian said, smiling. "You really did a great job. I'm jealous."

He picked up the paper, and there on the front page was his story. He had worked hard writing and rewriting it, and now here it was, in print. It was his most personal piece yet, and he was nervous about the reaction it would get.

He hadn't looked at the article for a few days, and he could hardly believe he had written it in the first place. He looked over it again, this time in print.

> Remember Anthony Camarata? If you are a typical St. Norbert's student, maybe you remember teasing him, or avoiding him. I knew Anthony. I picked on him just like you did. I hated him the same way everyone did. But one day, he invited me to come to his house, and that was when I learned the truth about the boy we all treated like dirt.
>
> This whole year I have written stories for *St. Norbert News* about miracles. I wrote about a weeping icon and about a couple of miraculous healings, and other things, too. But the most amazing miracle I've seen is the miracle of Anthony, who is a living saint.

Basil skimmed the rest of the article, which told the story of Anthony's dad, of Father Isaac's conversion, and about Anthony's father going to jail. It told about how Anthony was safe with his uncle. Reflecting on his words and on his first year at a new school, Basil could hardly believe everything that had happened. It was a monumental year in his life. He felt relieved, proud, and sad all at the same time that the year was over.

June

⚙ Chapter 31

IT WAS EARLY JUNE. The school year was over and the summer was already hot. The Saturday after the last day of class, Basil and his mother invited his *News* friends over for an end-of-the-year party.

After having pizza and ice cream in the house, Basil asked his mom if he and the kids could go for a hike over to the monastery. She said yes, so Basil called to get permission from Father Isaac. Then the kids rushed out back, Christian leading the way with Basil, Sarah, Abbie, and Shamus in tow.

"Let me show you all how to do this right," Christian said, full of confidence. "Now be careful, Shamus. Don't crush the delicate fauna with your careless stomping," she pretended to scold Shamus, winking at Basil.

"Don't crush the fauna," Shamus mimicked in a high-pitched voice as they tramped through the forest, laughing and joking all the way and having a great time. The burden of school days and starchy uniforms was well behind them, and they had only the freedom and joy of summer to look forward to.

They stopped in the clearing by the stream for a snack, sitting in the tall grasses of the meadow amid wildflowers of all colors. After they had all been munching in silence for a few minutes, they started chatting about the year, remembering the highlights.

"I don't know how we got through this year," said Basil. "This was the hardest school year of my life."

"I don't know how you got through the year, either," laughed Shamus. "I'm glad you're around, Basil."

"Thanks, Shamus," Basil said.

"Oh, hey, did you guys hear about Farley?" said Shamus.

"No, what happened?" Basil said.

"I heard that Farley told Marcus in religion class last Friday, after your article came out, that he was sorry he had ever teased Anthony," he said.

"Well," Abbie said, "Farley told me at a party the other day that he felt bad about always making fun of Anthony and Basil in class, and that he wants to help Basil with his articles next year. As long as there's a way to do it without ruining his reputation." The kids all laughed.

"Can you imagine Farley doing research?" Christian said. "The kid barely knows how to read! I don't think he's ever not cheated on a test in his life."

"I think that's the greatest miracle I've seen yet," Basil joked. Everyone laughed. He thought about it for a moment, and then added, "Farley can change. And maybe we can help him."

"Maybe you're right, Basil," Christian said. "We should give him a chance. I've learned better now that I know the truth about Anthony."

"Speaking of Anthony," Sarah said, "shouldn't we finish our hike to the monastery?"

"Yeah, let's go," Shamus said.

So they picked up their backpacks and trekked off through the woods in the waning summer afternoon.

About the Author:

Heather Zydek lives in Wauwatosa, Wisconsin, with her husband and three daughters. She is the editor of *The Revolution: A field manual for changing your world* and *The Relevant Nation: 50 Activists, Artists and Innovators who are changing their world through faith.* She enjoys reading, building snow forts, biking, and someday hopes to create a real secret garden.

Learn more about Heather's work at www.heatherzydek.com, or visit her website about this book at http://www.heatherzydek.com/basil.

Other Conciliar Press Books for Young Adults:

Ella's Story: The Duchess Who Became a Saint
by Maria Tobias, with illustrations by Bonnie Gillis

    Ella's Story brings to life the amazing journey of Princess Elizabeth, from privileged childhood to eventual martyrdom. While her biography, as St. Elizabeth the New Martyr, is available to adults, this is the first such book for girls, and is written in an approachable, appealing style. Maria Tobias tells the princess' story in such a lively way that the book is hard to put down. Elizabeth, a real princess, is gifted with all those qualities girls still seek (intelligence, beauty, wealth, renown), converts to Orthodoxy, and subsequently sheds all earthly glory for the greater prize of the martyr's crown. She is a true role model for today. A chapter book, with black-and-white illustrations.
Paperback, 80 pages (ISBN 1-888212-70-5) Order No. 006536 $8.95*

Saint Innocent: Apostle and Missionary
by Sarah Elizabeth Cowie

    If you close your eyes and think about Alaska, what do you see? Eskimos and igloos? Mountains of snow? Polar bears and icebergs? Do you know that not all Alaskan natives are Eskimos? There are many different tribes of native peoples. Each has its own language and way of life. Many of these native peoples have been Orthodox Christians for over two hundred years. This is largely due to the missionary efforts of one man, Saint Innocent of Alaska. He converted and baptized thousands of native people into the Christian faith. He was a wonderful and godly man who lived a missionary life full of adventures that you would never dream of! Many people believe he is the greatest Christian missionary of all time. A chapter book, with black-and-white illustrations.
Paperback, 104 pages (ISBN 1-888212-74-8) Order No. 006975 $10.95*

Keeper of the Light: Saint Macrina the Elder, Grandmother of Saints
by Bev. Cooke, with illustrations by Bonnie Gillis

    The road to sainthood takes a lifetime to travel. . . . Late in the fourth century, Christians are labeled enemies of the Roman Empire—hounded, arrested, tortured, and executed. Macrina and her husband Basil, once-wealthy Christians, flee with their small son to the mountainous forests south of the Black Sea. There, Macrina embarks on a seven-year journey of unexpected tests and trials that will take her through a harsh and hungry wilderness pilgrimage, only to plunge her into poverty and danger on the streets of Neocaesarea. So begins Macrina's adventure in faith, as she undertakes the process of becoming one of the most influential women in sacred history. Readers of all ages will be fascinated by the story of St. Macrina, who had a profound influence on her grandchildren—St. Basil the Great, St. Gregory of Nyssa, and St. Macrina the Younger. She is truly a great confessor of the Orthodox Christian faith. A chapter book, with black-and-white illustrations.
Paperback, 200 pages (ISBN 1-888212-77-2) Order No. 007106—$14.95*

---

* Prices listed were current as of March 1, 2007. Prices do not include applicable tax and postage & handling charges. Please call Conciliar Press at 800-967-7377 for complete ordering information, or to request a catalog of other Conciliar Press publications (books for younger children, books for adults, and more). Visit us at our website: www.conciliarpress.com.